The book is a skillful weaving of the concrete and the ephemeral and offers unflinching observations of the ugly and the beautiful. It visits the pits in order to know the heights. The author doesn't fall for the trap of holiness, of escape. Rather he is present—here, now, just as it is. He has the audacity, the courage really, to go beyond traditional truth.

Following his journey, I find my feet more fully present in my own journey. The book is a relief from the cacophony of defined spiritual paths and the message is sweet, sweet, sweet.

— Jane English, designer and illustrator of
Tao Te Ching (translated by Gia-fu Feng)

Invoking the spirits of crow and fish, Spivey seeks guidance in healing the wounded soul. In this journey across memory and mountains, he finds landmarks of meaning in his family stories of land and loss. This is a deeply honest look at how "drunks and sons of drunks" have added to the pain of landscape destruction. Spivey dreams not of retribution, but of restoration, of mind and land made whole, released from the grip of violence. An uncommon exploration of drink, love, and the call to dignity in all our relations. Spivey's writing is bold, authentic, and richly present with the fullness of the story he must tell.

—Stephanie Kaza, author, *The Attentive Heart*
Professor, University of Vermont

The Great Western Divide

The
Great Western
Divide

A History with Crow, Coyote, Chaos and God

John Spivey

CROWSCRY PRESS

Santa Barbara, California

The Great Western Divide
A History with Crow, Coyote, Chaos and God
By John Spivey

Published by:
CrowsCry Press
4732 Ashdale Street
Santa Barbara, California 93110

Copyright © 2006 by John Spivey

Excerpts from Lao Tsu, *Tao Te Ching*, translated by Gia-fu Feng and Jane English, copyright © 1972 by Gia-fu Feng and Jane English. Published by Vintage Books, a division of Random House, Inc., New York. Used by permission of Random House, Inc., and Jane English.

ISBN-13: 978-0-9765691-1-4

Library of Congress Control Number: 2005902538

Book and Cover Production by Christine Nolt, Cirrus Design,
Santa Barbara, California
Edited by Gail M. Kearns, To Press and Beyond,
Santa Barbara, California

Front cover credits: *Raven*, lithograph by Davis TeSelle.
davisteselle.com
Image edited by John Spivey using a fractal image from the
Mandelbrot Set.

Back cover credits: *Kaweah Lake,* woodcut by Tom Killion
from *The High Sierra of California*
tomkillion.com

For my grandparents,
Harry & Myrtle
and
My spiritual grandfathers,
Robert Blakemore
&
Robert A. Johnson

Contents

When men lack a sense of awe, there will be disaster.

—Lao Tsu
Tao Te Ching

Before a person sees the true nature of things, mountains are just mountains and rivers are just rivers; after a first glimpse into the truth of things, mountains are no longer mountains and rivers are no longer rivers; yet after enlightenment, mountains are once again mountains and rivers once again rivers.

—Paraphrased from a Zen Parable

Coyote Shows His Hand

We're going to talk about God here and that's a pretty dangerous thing to do. There's a great danger that we may not even be talking about the same thing, or even be on the same page. For the moment, though, I'll ask that you agree to just be here with me on this page and let the story unfold. Even if an infinite God is beyond naming and beyond attributes and beyond measurement, I'm still stuck with the name if you and I are going to communicate. Actually, God is a poor choice of words, but it's as good as any other. We're also going to talk about fear. You can't really investigate God without investigating fear.

I'm going to be like the magician who shows you the secrets behind his tricks and then still steps up and performs them anyway. I want to show you your intelligence, not what you learned in school, but your own deep sense of knowing. Strangely enough, in order to do that, I have to talk about myself and about the landscape in which I was raised. In the end, it's the only story I really know.

Everything you need to know is spread at your feet and scattered throughout your life. That's all I really have to say, but I'm going to take awhile to tell you about these things. This is not a passive story, but an interactive one. I want to cast my line and catch your mind, then have you turn, take over the story, and somehow make it your own. I want to inspire you to some deep feeling, but can't tell you what that feeling should be. Just sit with it and let it teach you. Let it be you that is walking the Great Valley and exploring the high peaks.

I could have called this an introduction, but then you wouldn't have read it. Storytellers do things like that.

The Great Western Divide

At this moment in our history of fear and in this present place we are called to stop and see clearly. It is the great act of being.

What is dream and what is real? What is spirit and what is of the mind? I have a story to tell and stories within stories. I'll light a fire and ask that we sit a while together.

It is almost dark and without warning I find myself aboard a fishing boat some thirty to thirty-five feet in length. We are headed out into the open sea. As I look around about the boat I notice two men standing at the stern silently fishing. I hold to my place in the background and without speaking to the men I somehow know that one of them is after some great fish. He seems intent, urgent. The fishing lines trail behind the boat while the sky darkens, the sea heaves and a storm begins to brew.

As the boat rolls on the large swells the fishing lines pay out with each surge of the water. The partner of this urgent man begins to notice the other man's line. There is a strange pull at the end of each surge which signals that there is something on the line. The urgent fisherman grabs the pole and starts to wind the reel as the other man goes to inspect the boat in the building storm.

The scene turns on itself and I suddenly become the man inspecting the fishing boat. I notice a few small leaks where caulk is breaking down near the portholes, but I'm not concerned. I picture in my mind what I need to do for the next time we put to sea. I move to the wheel and turn the boat toward home at full speed while my partner keeps on trying to land the great fish. In wonderment I try to imagine a kind of fish that can swim at the full speed of the boat and still fight with such strength and vigor. As we near the harbor the line suddenly goes slack and the fish is gone. After the intense struggle the fisherman is left empty-handed. All that he has to show for his foray into the dark is his memory and disappointment.

Again there is a shift. I am no longer the helmsman but the fisherman. As the boat is docked I leap out and race down the street. I come to a bookstore, run inside and excitedly try to tell my fish story of the one that got away. Suddenly I am aware that the spirit of the fish is with me, is inside me, inhabiting me. It tells me to take some paper and something to write with, that it will draw a picture of itself. I grab a piece of paper that is already covered with writing because I expect only a small scrawl in the corner. I pick up a pen, and then reject it. A pencil seems more appropriate for a drawing. The pencil *starts moving in my hand and the paper begins to rotate around a center point. The pencil moves back and forth across the paper like a stylus, and a picture begins to form. As the picture forms, the spirit tells me what is pictured is seven million years old. A great mass of something begins to appear on the page, but it conflicts with all the marks, smudges and writings that are already there. I stop, look around and find a clean sheet of paper and put it before me. As I do so I see that others around are watching my actions, waiting. I pray to the fish spirit to do it once more and I apologize for using the old, used and dirtied piece of paper. The page again begins to spin and again my hand and the pencil move. The same drawing starts to emerge. The entity seems as vast as the sea bottom, with innumerable appendages like an anemone. I think I see human faces in it, maybe all of humanity, maybe all of life.*

If one is willing to spend the time and energy, there is a great vista to be had from atop Moro Rock in the Sierra Nevada. Below to the south and west the flat fertile San Joaquin Valley meets the canyon of the Middle Fork of the Kaweah River. During the summer the area is a jumble of parched yellow hills and dark chaparral that periodically is held in years of long drought. The eye moves up the canyon to where three of the five forks of the Kaweah converge at Three Rivers—the North, South and Middle forks. Slightly more eastward the East Fork flows down from Mineral King and the

Marble Fork flows through Potwisha to meet the main body of the river. But all of this is lost from direct view within the folds of the hills. The river here at Moro Rock lies three to four thousand feet below, coursing through granite boulders, lined by oak forest. To the north are meadows surrounded by stands of Giant Sequoia. Black oaks flank the beginnings of the path up the great rock. The path becomes a stone staircase that follows folds and clefts, winds to the edge of the precipice and then winds back to another fold in the rock. Long before there was anything of a path or staircase, my great, great Uncle Will used to climb this rock with his farm rope and work boots. Across the canyon, Castle Rocks' turrets and spires thrust to the sky and seem to stand guard to the far reaches of the backcountry.

To the east is a line of jagged peaks of various shades of white and grey granite, their glacial polish catching the midday summer sun. This is the backcountry of the Great Western Divide. Sawtooth, Mt. Eisen, Lippincott Mountain, Eagle Scout Peak, Mt. Stewart, Triple Divide Peak. Whenever I stand on Moro Rock, there is a strange enticement to these peaks and my eye keeps returning to them over and over, never quite able to take it all in. The river has its most obvious source here. Between this point and the Great Western Divide, Mehrten Creek tumbles down the granite mountainside to the Kaweah. Behind the divide is the Kaweah Ridge. Mt. Kaweah, Kaweah Queen, Red Kaweah, Black Kaweah. Those names tumble through my mind and pull at the edge of something that I can never quite identify. What is it? The names seem to exist in a deep primal world of images that is always one step away from direct knowing. Some part of me senses that these depths exist in the records of the peaks and as the source of the snows, the moraines and cirques and the cascading Kaweah below. I also sense that the peaks somehow exist in the imagination of these primal depths. Beyond all the ridges, towering hidden and unseen is Mt. Whitney.

I was born and raised where the foothills meet the San Joaquin Valley there below. Dutch Bill Mehrten, my German great, great grandfather, settled in the foothills as a boy after the Gold Rush in 1854. He raised cattle and wheat, sold horses to the stagecoach lines. This country is so a part of me that I sometimes think if you were to take a cross section of my brain and study all of its convolutions, its whorls and ridges, that it would look surprisingly like these Sierra foothills with all of its manzanita and oak, its granite and yellowed grasses. The Great Western Divide looms as the source of all that sustains and defines this terrain of mind. What has it divided and what has it provided? The Kaweah runs through my mind. Where has it started and where does it go?

Here

I see that the fire is beginning to catch. I'll add a few sticks to get it going. Fire, stolen from the gods, or maybe it was really a gift. Fire leaps out in the darkness. What does it bring to this world? Just sit, just watch. Come to the answer.

Do you know where you come from, the landscape of your origin? Would you be able to somehow show me that landscape? How did you get to this place? Is that place really here?

The Dusty Feather of Flight

Great red rocks tower over the Santa Ynez
and the ancient spirits of time and place seem
as real as the stone.
Young people come here restless to party and drink,
then climb the red towers and
throw themselves down to the river,
barely missing the rocks.
Some do not miss.
A few hundred feet away we walk the dirt road
lined with sedimentary rock and white sage,
and by the road
a redtail, dead from some unknown cause.
I kneel, turn it over,

gently pluck a long feather from its wing
to hand to my daughter.
Keep this, I say, it is an omen,
a gesture from the spirits to you.
Behind us the young ones throw themselves down
over and over
desperately seeking the sensation of flight.
Here is the dusty way, its creatures,
its gifts,
this poem a feather.

Let's begin this story in a boat offshore, suspended over the depths. Behind us the island has fallen away as we head into the Santa Barbara Channel. A container ship bound northward, probably for San Francisco, has raised a wake that will soon become a tossing swell on the island's beaches and within the sea caves that pock the shoreline. We have just been on Santa Cruz Island where a high fog now caps the peaks, obscuring them from view. Overhead the sky is clearing as evening comes on. The mainland ahead, though, is shrouded in deep marine layer. Suddenly the ocean around begins to come alive as thousands of common dolphins surround the boat and swim with us, surfing the stern and bow wakes with playful joy. Two-foot juveniles swim alongside full-grown mothers arching gracefully through the rolling seas.

The Chumash tell stories of how they once lived on Santa Cruz in a world of plenty. After a while their fresh water dried up and their fisheries collapsed. After they prayed to their gods the gods granted them deliverance via a rainbow bridge to the mainland. They were not to look down. Of course, some did and they fell into the ocean far below. Their relatives prayed once more, this time for the fallen. The gods once more responded, changing the drowning tribes folk into dolphins.

My thoughts swim with the Chumash changelings alongside the boat and through the wake. I've been traveling with my students and other faculty for eight days and we are coming home. Rites of passage exist in many cultures, but not in ours. In many native cultures children are just children till comes the day. At twelve or thirteen, others of the tribe kidnap them and take them away from their parents to learn the larger things from elders. Our school does this, takes the kids away three times a year to begin to connect with greater mystery and greater knowledge.

We have traversed the backcountry of the Santa Ynez Mountains following the course of the Santa Ynez River from Lake Cachuma to its source on the Murietta Divide and then down the Matilija River to Ojai. This trip to the island has been our last exploration before heading home. It has all been good, and yet there is something more for me to teach as well as something more for me to learn. I've not yet been able to truly pass on all that I have learned so far. How can I explain the ways in which these changelings of the ocean's depths extend to the snow shrouded peaks, how the senseless makes sense and that there is a feast in the midst of famine? I still carry the burden of this story that is untold and I know that there is even more life to live in the telling.

Jonah of the Bible carried a story that he refused to tell, was storm tossed then swallowed by the great fish of the depths. I am Jonah, the storm and the great fish. I pray to the fish spirit once more to tell its story. Let the storms cease and the picture emerge. We cannot live as islands any longer but must make it to the mainland. There is purpose to the life there. We must restore the fisheries as we probe the depths. Don't look down.

I'm walking down the hallway of my grandparent's farmhouse. It seems so very real that I know as I'm walking that this is a lucid dream. I know somehow this is now my house to dwell in. As I walk through the kitchen and into the dining room I see there is no table as I remember. I know, however, that I have the skill to build a table of my own design from which food can be served. I enter the living room and the scene starts to fade. I try to hold on to the dream, but only for a moment, then it is gone.

I arrived in Santa Barbara through strange and mysterious circumstances. Years ago I returned to the San Joaquin Valley, where I grew up, for a high school reunion. It was the twenty-fifth and a two-day event. I almost chose not to go because my life was in such disarray and my spirit had begun to collapse. Something impelled me to extend, to inwardly push out against the collapse into depression. I had to choose to not be ruled by my sense of disgrace. My route took me across the San Joaquin Delta and down the Valley of the San Joaquin from where I lived north of the San Francisco Bay. As I pulled into the blacktopped parking lot of the reunion, a woman pulled into the place along side me. I looked over and recognized her as an old classmate. We said hello, then passed on by.

The next day I drove the ten miles to visit the graves of my grandparents in the shadow of the Sierra foothills. This is a ritual every time I come back home. I sat at their graves in silence and contemplation, reviewing the successes and failures of my life to date. My grandfather was old Dutch Bill's grandson, born in 1891, native to this place. My grandmother was born in Iowa, and then moved to Oklahoma. She used to make the church rounds with her Methodist circuit-riding father as he traveled through the Indian reservations of the territory before statehood. They later moved to Hanford at the upper end of Tulare Lake.

As a youth, my grandfather drove cattle to summer forage in the High Sierra, worked eighteen-hour days in the fields harvesting wheat. He always wanted to be a writer, but Uncle Will made him quit school after eighth grade to work on the farm. I used to work next to him in the fields and listen to his stories. In all those years, though, he never told me what he had truly wanted to say. My grandparents were married for about sixty-five years. As I sat silently at their graves, a moment of clear certainty occurred and, in that moment, I knew I would spend the rest of my life with my classmate. And that is what has happened. It happened without drama or striving, like a smooth flow of continuity in a fractured world. It seems that my greatest pain and my greatest gifts have come in that landscape.

Though I live in a paradise that many desire, I am not yet home. I will not be home till the telling of this story is complete. The range of the Great Western Divide still stretches across my mind, beckoning. There is a pull toward the place of my ancestry, the place that matches the terrain of my mind. I remember the hills that started two miles from my house and rose above the vineyards and orchards. I remember winter vistas of the granite snowy crest out our front window and the familiar knob of Homer's Nose protruding on the ridgeline. And there is something more indefinable to the pull, the pull of some inchoate vision amid this landscape that lives and breathes somewhere inside me. I am like a salmon that is strangely pulled back to the stream of its origin guided by the smell of another world. Though you can never enter the same river twice, the river is always there, even if only in memory. Is the river the banks that guide it or is the river its contents of water and life? Going to the source is really not a journey to death but one of discovering the true nature of life.

Santa Barbara, where we now live, is a place of comfort and safety, but its geography as yet does not align with my mind. The sea is rarely turbulent like near Big Sur or Mendocino. The Channel Islands, twenty-five miles offshore, create a buffer to the greater Pacific Ocean and the wild chaos of its weather and waves. The mountains here are chaparral covered with mostly sandstone and are only three thousand to thirty-five hundred feet tall. There are no rivers except at storm time. The mountains rise steeply behind the town and the rain of winter storms quickly rushes down the mountainside gullies into streams that rise to flood stage within hours and pour out through the myriad concrete-lined creeks along the coastline. They pour directly into the sea without the cushion of the wetlands that were once deemed useless, and so filled. Within days the flow is gone once again. I dream of year-round rivers that cascade through granite, oxygenated and trout-filled.

We live in a tract house surrounded by neighbors and

legions of cars. It's not easy for me to live amid such feature-less domestication. I have always lived close to the border between the Conscious and Unconscious, between the land of what we think we know and the deep sea of all that really is. I am pulled toward the nameless that for me has a face.

To Get There from Here

Stories exist within stories like eternally reflecting parallel mirrors that stand facing each other. I could tell you stories about this fire before us, but are they the fire? If your house once burned down you might feel fear and anger staring into these flames. If you found haven at a stranger's fire on a cold wintry night you might feel warm and safe. What do you see, what do you see?

A friend once told me a story that he said came from some midwestern woodland tribe. In this tale a boy who was to become a man was sent from the village into the farthest depths of the forest alone to hunt. He was told that as he walked further and further into the forest, passing from unknown into unknown, that he would eventually meet the Demon of the Forest. Now this Demon could surprise him from any direction and its face was grotesque and fearsome. The boy was neither to run from it nor attack it. Instead, he had to invite it to sit at his fire with him and offer it food. He had to sit across the fire from the Demon the entire night while unflinchingly watching its horrible face. If the boy were successful the Demon would reveal the deep secret of the forest. If the boy failed at his task the Demon would lay waste to the boy's family and village over and over again. This Demon has visited my family repeatedly and I may be the first to meet its gaze. This story I tell will see me through the night.

There is a character in the lore of the Northwest called Always-Living-at-the-Coast, who is Coyote's father-in-law. But all of us, no matter where we live, are always living at the coast, living at the border between the land and the depths with Coyote somewhere in the picture. Our effluent of fear and desire flow out across the surface of the sea in a great black slick. Any being that rises from the depths to our world will be encrusted with this dark toxic waste. All we will see of the gift of knowledge is our own black face of fear.

It's not an easy task or a direct route to get back to the Kaweah watershed from Santa Barbara. There is no direct easterly route through the Santa Ynez coastal range or through the Tehachapis. In one of those oddities of location, Santa Barbara lies on a stretch of coast and mountains that run from east to west. It is surrounded by the sea to the south and by mountains in all other directions. At Santa Barbara the coastline swings in a southeasterly direction. In order to go north, one has to drive west for thirty minutes. In order to go east, one has to drive south for forty-five minutes. Either way eventually leads to Interstate 5. By going south to Ventura (San Buenaventura) then east, one intersects I-5 in the middle of the Tehachapi Mountains at the northern boundary of Los Angeles (Nuestra Senora la Reina de Los Angeles).

The southern tip of the Sierra Nevada Range drops down to the town of Tehachapi at the entry to the Mojave Desert. The Tehachapi Mountains then rise and circle the southern end of the San Joaquin Valley and meet the coastal range in a great U-shape. Interstate 5 proceeds to the north through these mountains where the earth buckles and heaves with sudden up-thrusts, exposing the sedimentary strata at acute angles. The landscape is so rugged and covered with such dense chaparral that the Spanish explorers penetrated it only with great difficulty. In spring some of the hillsides are covered with vast carpets of golden poppies and blue-purple lupine, the way much of California appeared in the early nineteenth century. An apocryphal family story tells of one German family named Poppe that intermarried with the Mehrtens. Their holdings were said to be so vast and covered with the golden wildflowers that the plant was named after them.

Interstate 5 passes near Mt. Pinos whose 8900-foot peak sports winter snow even in this desert, a place that I occasionally go to ski the backcountry of the high Pinon forest. From the peak are views from the Pacific to the San Joaquin Valley. At Fort Tejon the interstate suddenly swoops down the Grapevine Grade through Grapevine Canyon (Canada de las Uvas), named for its numerous wild vines in more primal times, named even earlier Portosuelo de Cortes in honor of the conqueror. When I-5 was a two-lane curving highway, the descent could be terrifying. Trucks routinely lost their brakes and plunged off the road. My truck-driving father once took that long ride without brakes, barely managing to make it to the valley floor safely.

There is the long steep grade of the Grapevine and then suddenly the world is flat, flat as far north as the eye can see and beyond. The Great Valley extends all the way to the volcanic cone of Mt. Shasta near the Oregon border in this unrelieved flatness. It is an abrupt transition to the land of Yokuts

Homochu, "Southland" in the language of the original Yokuts inhabitants. Pedro Fages, the first white man to explore the area would have seen a much different vista. The great flatness is the Tulare Plain. Once this great Valley of the San Joaquin was called Valle de los Tulares (Valley of the Tules), whose centerline was an interconnected spine of lakes and sloughs and rivers all making their slow murky way north, in the only direction they could go, to the San Francisco Bay. All of the waterways along this spine of the valley were choked dense growths of nettles, wormwood, grapevines, willows, cottonwoods, hemp, oak, ash, bay laurel and tules. I can see in my mind's eye the dense flights of migratory waterfowl exploding in a thunderous rush from the surface of the lake, the redwing and tricolor blackbirds among the tules and the tule elk wading in the shallows. During the Gold Rush, cannons of birdshot would be pointed at the sky to bring down hundreds of waterfowl in a blast, all to be sold to hungry miners. This tangled eruption of life extended for hundreds of miles from below Bakersfield north to the San Francisco Bay in a swath up to twenty miles wide. The swath was virtually impenetrable except in times of low water. Driving cattle from San Francisco to Placerville, an eastward hundred-mile journey as the crow flies, required a 750-mile detour to the south to Bakersfield and then north again at times of high water.

Valle de los Tulares. Motorists hurry from one end of the valley to the other on Interstate 5 now, anxious to depart from this featureless plain of alkali flats and corporate farms. They hope the wind doesn't suddenly come across the flats and kick up the fine alkali dust in blinding storms across the roadway. It can leave a chain reaction of death and twisted metal. In winter a dense bank of tule fog hangs close to the ground seeking out the waterways it once embraced. Tule fog without the tules, without the scurry and tangle of life. Like the dust storms the now silent and seemingly sullen fog visits death on the roadways, a revenge of sorts.

Below the Grapevine the highway splits at a point south of where the old marshy waterways began. Interstate 5 goes up the western side of the old Valle de los Tulares avoiding almost all towns and civilization and traversing the alkali flats, corporate farms and a reeking cattle feed lot or two. The interstate also parallels the concrete lined California Aqueduct that seeks to drain the far north of California and paradoxically bring water back to this region in some more orderly fashion. The highway skirts the Kettleman Hills and catches the edge of tiny Kettleman City. During the mid-nineteenth century the newly arrived Kettelmanns had also intermarried with the newly arrived Mehrtens, all immigrants direct from Germany and trying to survive on this strange complex frontier. They brought their old ways to the new land, a seemingly chaotic world in need of order and predictability.

State Highway 99 goes to the right at the fork in the interstate. The highway takes a route more directly up the center of the Valley and a little toward the eastern foothills that become the Sierra Nevada. To the east of the present Highway 99, the old highway can be seen intermittently lined with trees. When I travel through I can see the old buildings that housed the old truck stops and greasy spoon cafes, places where the parking lots used to fill with big rigs, the drivers checking out tires and brakes for the haul over the Grapevine and on into Los Angeles. In Bakersfield the highway crosses over the sandy riverbed of the Kern River. The Kern also has its source up below the Kaweah Peaks in the shadow of Red Kaweah, Black Kaweah and Kaweah Queen. The Kern cascades its whitewater way through Class IV and Class V rapids down a circuitous route along the southeastern flank of the Sierra, rounds the southern tip of the mountains, heads westward into the Valley and then goes nowhere. The river once flowed through the Buena Vista Slough to the southern end of the vast Tulare Lake in the center of the Valle de los Tulares, a lake that at times would measure eighty to a hundred miles in length. Now that the lake no longer exists, the river runs to nothingness, no longer able to push north to the San Joaquin River and on out through the Golden Gate to the Pacific. My mind always catches on the incompleteness, that the snowy promise of the high granite peaks no longer has the chance to run through to the sea.

In 1983, when El Nino played havoc with the weather of the Pacific Coast, there was a strange reversal of fortune. Amid the El Nino-fueled downpours, Tulare Lake threatened to rise from the dead and reclaim its legacy. The corporate farmers who now squatted on the old lakebed appealed to President Reagan for help, so the water was pumped northward at taxpayer expense into the drainage of the San Joaquin River and out through the Delta and the San Francisco Bay. The lake stirs to life with every El Nino-powered deluge, the masses of birds instinctively flying home by the thousands, but the lake is soon strangled back into submission by the network of pumps, levees and dikes.

Highway 99 north of Bakersfield is lined on both sides with dusty fields, some bearing, some abandoned, the old trees and vines seeming tortured in their neglect. Almonds and pistachios give way to grapes with giant weeds protruding through the row tops. Fallow fields grow green tumbleweeds that still hold to the ground. A maximum-security state prison sits along the western side of the highway, its exercise yard exposed and barren in summer's blast furnace sun.

Off to the west is the small dry town of Alpaugh, which used to be an island in the middle of Tulare Lake inhabited by the Wowol, later called Atwell Island. During the summer the air is dry, hot and dusty hazy. Smog blankets the Great Valley so that the air is nearly as yellow dense as in Los Angeles. The Sierra and its granite peaks cannot be seen. Much is truly lost from view.

I have seen signs sprout along the roadway near the neglected fields, signs that proclaim a world view where little can be seen any longer, a Burma shave litany of belief.

> IRS means
> In
> Range
> Shoot

and,

> Believe in Jesus or
> Go To Hell.

This is some great irony. I have believed in Jesus and I've also lived through Hell.

The Crow Cry People

In this flickering fire I can see black swirling shapes. The sparks also swirl and carry skyward. The shapes separate and cry out. They coalesce and fall back into the fire and then downward into coals. Did you hear them? The dark shapes in the darkness cry to be heard. I will continue.

The Buddhist monk Thich Nhat Hanh uses the telephone to help awaken himself. Like a temple bell, the ring of the phone is a reminder to come back to who he really is, to be present in this very moment. I use crows. Sometimes solitary crows fly overhead and alight in one of the trees around our tract house. Sometimes there are roving gangs of demonic birds that flock to our trees, torment the cats and demand attention. As they soar about, then flare their wings and settle to a branch, their sudden "Caw!" pierces me, brings me to myself and to something deep, dark and mysterious. Sometimes in that piercing moment there is a shift and two realities overlap and in that moment I live in both. It isn't one or the other but just, "Caw!" "Yes!" In that moment exists a knowledge of that which I have sought, but also an awareness of that which I'd rather not know. Much of the great secret of the forest lies in that which I'd rather not know. Crows are not kind, they just are.

Such are the *corvidae*, the family of crows and ravens, blue jays and magpies. They would rob you blind as much as teach you to see. Some scientists think that these corvids are nearly as smart as the higher apes. I have rescued wounded adult crows and floundering juveniles, held them in my hand and looked them in the eye. Always there is the sense of someone looking back, studying me.

Clarence King was one of the first white men to explore the Sierra Nevada and the first person to map the Great Western Divide. He was employed by the State Geologist Josiah Whitney to survey the new state. In return King named Mt. Whitney in his boss' honor. In his classic *Mountaineering in the Sierra Nevada*, King wrote,

> *Visalia is the name of a small town embowered in oaks upon the Tulare Plain in Middle California, where we made our camp one May evening of 1864.*
>
> *Professor Whitney, our chief, the State Geologist, had sent us out for a summer's campaign in the High Sierras, under the lead of Professor William H. Brewer, who was more sceptical than I was as to the result of the mission.*
>
> *Several times during the previous winter Mr. Hoffman and I, while on duty at the Mariposa gold-mines, had climbed to the top of Mt. Bullion, and gained, in those clear January days, a distinct view of the High Sierra, ranging from the Mt. Lyell group many miles south to a vast pile of white peaks, which from our estimate, should lie near the heads of the*

King's and Kaweah rivers. Of their great height I was
fully persuaded; and Professor Whitney, on the
strength of those few observations, commissioned us to
explore and survey the new Alps.

. . . A stroke of good fortune completed our outfit
and my happiness by bringing to Visalia a Spaniard
who was under some manner of financial cloud. His
horse was offered for sale, and quickly bought for me
by Professor Brewer. We named him Kaweah, after the
river and its Indian tribe. He was young, strong, fleet,
elegant, a pattern of fine modeling in every part of his
bay body and fine black legs; every way good, only
fearfully wild, with a blaze of quick electric light in his
dark eye.

Shortly after sunrise one fresh morning we made a
point of putting the packs on very securely, and, getting
into our saddles, rode out toward the Sierras.

The group of farms surrounding Visalia is
gathered within a belt through which several natural,
and many artificial, channels of the Kaweah flow.
Groves of large, dark foliaged oaks follow this irrigated
zone; the roads, nearly always in shadow, are flanked
by small ranch-houses, fenced in with rank jungles of
weeds and rows of decrepit pickets.

There is about these ruins, these specimens of
modern decay, an air of social decomposition not
pleasant to perceive. Freshly built houses, still untinted
by time, left in rickety disorder, half finished windows,
gates broken down or unhinged, and a kind of sullen
neglect staring everywhere. What more can I say of the

*people than that they are chiefly Southern immigrants
who subsist upon pork?*

*. . . Our backs were now turned to this farm-belt,
the road leading us out upon the open plain in our
first full sight of the Sierras.*

Visalia. The city sits on Mill Creek, one of the four main
divisions of the Kaweah River when it enters the Great Valley
and forms the Kaweah Delta. When I say it sits on Mill Creek
it literally does, for the creek now travels foolishly confined
beneath the city. I remember the floods of 1956 when it
seemed that the rains would never stop and how the river
came up from below the city and submerged it as if the river
had lain in wait. From a child's point of view it seemed to last
an eternity. That was before they built the dam up there on the
Kaweah to protect the city from its own foolishness.

This place at one time was the land of the Yokuts, a people that once covered the entire valley. Here at Visalia was a village of the Talumne tribe, Watot Shulul. If you drive through
the streets of Visalia, every once in a while you'll come upon a
giant valley oak standing in the middle of the street, a vestige
of the great oak forest that once spread for many miles in every
direction. The trees once towered here and the original people
lived along the open flowing streams. I have read that the first
words that the Yokuts children learned were the names of the
birds that clamored through the treetops, birds like woodpecker and raven and crow. There were also wood duck and
magpie and many more. The woodpecker was *Pah-dah-dut*,
named for his incessant hammering. The blue jay planted the
oak trees, the wood duck won all of his colors from the crea-

tures of the forest in a game and the magpie taught the Yokuts to speak. The oak forests were cut for firewood and fence posts and to provide charcoal for the great iron locomotives.

I never knew these things growing up. Our farm was the farm and had always been the farm, a place with no history. When my father was out of work he sometimes cut firewood for sale. There were times I would help and we would fell some great oak tree in the middle of a pasture that the farmer wanted out of the way. It seemed as if it was always in the fall or winter and the acrid tannic smell of the burning brush and slash would mix with the dense tule fog and hang close around like a pungent ghost of the old marshland. Occasionally the sharp cry of a black crow penetrated the gray fog. "Caw!" In Yokuts, "Gaw!", their name for crow. The word for cry was "weah." "Gaweah," the cry of the crow, or crow cry. The Gaweah, the Crow Cry People, the only quarrelsome tribe of the Yokuts living in the Kaweah River Delta. The Yokuts prided themselves on living in harmony, whether in tribe or in family, and then there were the Gaweah as noisy and quarrelsome as crows. They were like dark shadows flapping, swarming about the landscape. Gaweah, Kaweah. Red Kaweah, Black Kaweah, Kaweah Queen. Those names cry out for attention, they try to bring something to the forefront of the mind. There are things that I've seen that I'd rather not know. Maybe I don't use crows. It could be that the crows use me.

Highway 198, the Mineral King Highway, goes directly east from Visalia to the Sierra. It's now a four-lane limited access highway, meaning that it's bound on both sides by a chain-link fence. This is where antelope once roamed freely. When I was a kid it was a two-lane roadway crossable at any point by kids on bicycles or farmers on their tractors. Now as the farmers would say, you have to go 'round your elbow to get to your thumb.

Five miles from Visalia and somewhere a little south of the highway was a burial mound. Dawau Nashid. The Bank of Italy (now the Bank of America) acquired it in 1930, then leveled it to plant alfalfa. There were over one thousand burials inside. Nearby is Linnell Camp, a camp for migrant workers. I don't know its condition today but in my youth the farm workers lived there in Grapes of Wrath squalor, and Peace Corps workers practiced there before going to third world countries. This county is now the poorest in the state with plumbingless shacks sprouting up at the edges of some of the towns.

It's farmland around this area still, though Visalia is eating it up quickly. There were sixteen thousand when I left in 1964 and over ninety thousand now. All through the valley the cities engulf the farmland. Soon, they say, houses and streets will cover over maybe a million acres of the richest farmland in the world. Visalia has always existed with an unbridled growth mentality, a vestige of its days as the main trading center between Stockton and Los Angeles. Modern inhabitants still reflexively respond to their unrecognized frontier urges to dominate the region. A scientist friend of mine noted while touring China he never saw any wild birds. They were a victim of unbridled human growth. The only birds that existed were in cages in the markets and people kept them as pets for luck. No wood duck with all its colors, no woodpecker incessantly hammering, no blue jay to plant the oaks, no magpie to teach the people to speak and no crow to taunt the people into knowing. This is the fruit of the unexamined urge toward growth.

The highway passes through a remaining stand of valley oaks near where I grew up. It's an oak preserve now but it's lost something over the years. There's a shallow sandy bottomed creek here, one of those fractalizations of the Kaweah that ends up in smaller and smaller channels till it becomes an irrigation furrow in some alfalfa field or vineyard or orchard. The remaining oaks look lonely, like maybe the few surviving Yokuts did as they looked around and wondered where all of the others went. There are fewer trees than I remember and there used to be wild grapevines hanging from the branches and thickets along the sandy stream banks. I remember helping to cut up an oak near this place that my father had felled in a pasture. My father did what he did and I followed. In not knowing the place or its history we little understood ours. Without truly knowing the past we could have no vision for the future of this place and no hope or vision for ourselves.

The crows still circle, land and call from the tops of the old oaks asking for what is due. I hear their scratchy, ratcheting laughter.

The Place of No History

History. What does it mean to have no history? History is just the path that we have walked and our ancestors have walked to get here. Good, bad, fearful, pleasant. Doesn't matter. History is not for the sake of mere judgment. True history is for just seeing. Your path may wind across the desert or deep into this forest blackness. As the path moves across the face of this great planet it also traces arcs around the sun and through the greater cosmos. Even in the face of all that, if you really know your history, you will know where you are. If you know where you are, then you will know how to get to the place where you need to go.

What do you remember? Who are you? Where do you come from? Is there a place that truly beckons you?

I am walking across the back rows of our old vineyard and aware that we no longer own this farm, but I don't really care that I'm trespassing. In fact I know that in reality the vineyard no longer exists anyway. As I walk along the rows I examine the bunches of grapes for their ripeness. As I get closer and closer to the

Mineral King Highway, the bunches become larger and the individual grapes become larger with deeper shades of purple black ripeness. I begin to sample them. The taste is exquisite. The seeds blend in with the flesh in both taste and color. When I am only a few rows from the highway I turn and grandfather suddenly appears. He is only in his fifties, strong, very present and mentally alert. He smiles and tells me that he has been growing these grapes for me.

Directly north of Exeter next to the Mineral King Highway stands a farmhouse. It has been randomly remodeled without much thought or vision over the years. Two giant fruitless mulberry trees once stood in the front yard providing needed shade from the hot summers. Now it stands there naked in the hot summer sun. Thirty feet to the north of the house is a well. It dips deep into the aquifer, fed by snowmelt that has tumbled down the Kaweah then seeped into the porous earth beneath the marshy delta. The water was as soft and fresh as snowmelt, clear and refreshing. The farm comprised ten acres of emperor grapes, now gone, replaced by horse pasture. The surrounding level land is no longer vineyards and orchards of peaches and plums, but orange groves.

During my youth a flow of excess capital began to make its way into this area when prosperous Los Angelinos enriched by a thriving aerospace industry found the need to invest their money. Everyone wanted to plant oranges. That was what they knew was profitable and that was what they wanted. Over time everything seemed to become oranges and it became a great monotony of monoculture. In the spring the area was once a checkerboard of pink blossoming peaches and white blossoming plums with dark red leaves, grapes pushing their new canes with new green leaves and majestic groves of walnuts, the white English walnut limbs protruding from their black walnut trunks. If one crop failed the others would carry the day. Now it is all boom or bust, oranges or nothing, at the mercy of the weather and market.

I am no great fan of orange groves. The earth surrounding the trees is packed and hardened and nothing else grows there due to the trees own potency and, before herbicides, the brown-black stains of weed oil, a means of checking the unbridled chaos of too many things growing. The groves used to always smell of the oil. The tilled soil and clumps of weeds in the vineyards and orchards housed rabbit, coveys of quail and bright exotic ring-necked pheasants from China. The orange groves sustain no life other than oranges.

In earlier times, Exeter was the self proclaimed Emperor Grape Capitol of the World, but the emperor is now a relic doomed not only by oranges, but also by the country's taste for seedless grapes, doomed by the seeds of their own fulfillment. No seedless variety can compare to the fullness and depth of the old seeded grapes. My grandfather would pluck grapes from the vines as we worked together, crunch the grapes, seeds and all, then say, "That's where all the iron is you know."

This is my old home, the place with no history. I didn't know growing up that the landscape wasn't always flat, that it once was an undulating landscape of hog wallows away from the marsh, a rolling plain like the Serengeti with an abundance of wildlife. The undulations moved eastward toward the Sierra where two miles away is the beginning of a long sloping hill. It begins at the Mineral King Highway and slopes upward toward the south till it becomes Rocky Hill, a jumble of oak and pictograph-covered granite. This is where the Sierra begin. The long ridge was called *Hawshau Shido*, "the Paint Place," where the Yokoda band of Yokuts mined a white earth for pigment. Now it's Badger Hill, lined with estates stretched across the great view of the high country that looms beyond. Rocky Hill was called *Chahkah Shahnau*, "Live Oak Place". My youth was governed by this presence, Hawshau Shido, Chahkah Shahnau and the Sierra. Maybe this presence was like God looking over my shoulder, a presence so taken for granted that it slipped from conscious thought. Maybe that is how I survived my youth where I was suspended in the momentary eternity of my own personal pain, my personal hell, ignorant of the greater story all around me. Now the snowy, granite mountains proper can rarely be seen through the smog haze, the power of their deliverance lost from sight and mind.

So I grew up in the shadow of the Paint Place and in the shadow of my father. My father was a southerner from North Carolina who liked his pork, and our house had something of the air of social decomposition, at least in my mind. Projects were started and nothing was ever finished. You see, my father was a drunk. Not a social or happy drunk, but one who at times would sleep in his own vomit. It wasn't always that way, but that's the way it ended. I remember nothing of my first five years except for being told that I put pots on my head and ran into the walls. Our family lived in North Carolina for a year when I was five. We lived near piney, swampy woods that lurked with the threat of copperheads and water moccasins. I feared to trail my hand in the water because of the stories of what lie beneath. It was here that my sister was born. Sort of. On that night my father was out sleeping with another woman, and my sister took her first breath while still inside the womb. But of course there was no possibility for another. She also took a shit. So she was born asphyxiated, almost brain dead and swathed in her own shit. She existed for three years. My father the southern fundamentalist assumed the mantle of his judgment. This is where the drinking started in earnest.

A half-mile to the south of our farm my grandfather and grandmother's farm embraced orchards and vineyards with rose gardens broken with lupine and poppy. The farmhouse existed in neglect for years after my grandfather sold it. Paint peeled from the neglected wooden double hung windows. Gone were the rose gardens and my grandfather's personal little orchard along the side of the house. Mechanical equipment got parked where the vegetable garden once was. Grandfather was careful to keep the equipment and messy fuel and oil at the barn far away from the house. Part of the farm was subdivided and several tract style houses built with fighting cocks tethered to stakes out front. All of the detritus of farming fell back into too small an area around the old house and I think that my grandfather's German sense of order would have been offended. It was as if my father's kind had taken over the countryside with no perception of beauty or the creation of beauty, conscious only of pain but not history.

Now it is all gone. One time I drove down the road as I always do when I return to this place, my eye searching for my grandparent's house. Gone, all gone without a trace. No orchard that he pruned and tended with devotion, not one tree left that he had tended with his hand, no house that he had built for his family in 1936. In the middle of the peach and plum orchards, there had once been a giant spreading walnut tree that stood next to the old chicken house. It had seemed to me like the tree of life. A great new sprawling mansion of a house now spreads across the field, and around the house acres of newly planted orange trees sprout from featureless sterile ground. For the new owners it is all a place of no history, the land once again leveled and scraped of its story. All that is left of my grandparents is their memory and a few incised characters in the granite of their tombstones. Just that, and the form and substance that helped give me seeing and my life.

In my dreams I have constantly returned to my grandparent's farmhouse like a spirit. I have looked all around the old farm and through the old house. I have yearned to be able to afford, reclaim and restore their old farm to its abundant wealth in the shadow of the Sierra.

I have struggled to understand the nature of chaos and order, find the overlap of worlds. There was only one time that my father found peace and that was when he was fishing. Like the Fisher King of myth he existed somewhere between living and dying, in too much pain to live, unable to die. Finally he succeeded. In dying that is. Once, after a week of his drinking, my mother walked into the kitchen and found him leaning over the counter, a drink in his hand. She touched him and he slid to the floor. I received a call at six in the morning, the pastor saying, "Your father is dead." I cried as I drove from LA to San Francisco up I-5 past the old dry, dead lakebed, all the while thinking, "You bastard, you died before I could find the secret that would heal you."

We used to go deep-sea fishing, the whole family together, making the trek across the San Joaquin Valley to the Central Coast. The Yokuts followed about the same route to the coast to trade with the Chumash for abalone, pismo clam, keyhole limpet and periwinkle shells. They skirted the northern shore of Tulare Lake in the middle of the valley, the lake full of fat lake trout and a few sturgeon swimming among the tules. Maybe a few salmon. As we traveled I could see in the southern distance a silver reflection of all that remained of the lake. So we'd cross this ghost of a lakebed and head to the coast. I can imagine the spirits of the fish swimming a few feet over the surface of the dry, dusty alkaline valley looking for something, maybe someone.

We'd fish at Morro Bay and I can remember slipping out past the great rock in the gray fog at dawn. We always caught fish. If I hooked a big one my father would never trust me; he'd take the pole from my hands and fight the fish in himself. I never learned to succeed by successful progressions of small failures. Once I caught a forty-pound, fifty-inch white sea bass, the largest they'd seen in years. Took my dad 45 minutes to land it. The last time we went fishing there I was 17 and ready to go off to college. We went for albacore, the most beautiful fish that I'd ever seen, all streamlined and silver. It hits your line like a ton of bricks. I hooked one or two, and then mutely and by reflex handed the pole to him.

In my mind I see him in his last days sitting in a small boat on the San Pablo Bay at the mouth of the San Joaquin, fishing for sturgeon and stripers in the fog, alone and unreachable. He is buried near where the San Joaquin Delta meets the San Francisco Bay, where the Kaweah might end if it could.

I am deep-sea fishing with my brother and my father. We are fishing for albacore but have caught nothing. As the boat heads back I see a flash of silver down deep and know that there are indeed albacore, but no one believes me. My line is tangled with all the lines from the boat. I begin to thread through them all so that I can land the fish. Suddenly I find myself standing on the shore with my brother. I am still landing the fish, and all the other lines have dropped away. While standing on a small spit of land that extends into the bay, I start to land the albacore to my left but as I step into the water I am shocked by an electric eel. The fish moves to my right and I begin to land it. As it comes out from the water it looks like a red snapper, much smaller than an albacore and I don't understand it. At this moment all of the other men from the boat, ten to twelve of them, approach and prepare to ritually divide the fish. The fish becomes more like a hawk with red feathers and it stands with its wings outstretched and looks to the left. I feel sorry for this creature and want to set it free, but notice that the ends of its fin/wings have been broken. Someone stuffs a rag down its throat to stifle its scream.

The Fisher King

Imagine as you sit there across the fire that you are a child, that you are burned by the coals, and you cry out in pain, yet I continue the story. You cry out once more and I continue the story. Soon, in futility, you make no sound but the cry still echoes in your ears. Soon the only story is the cry.

Some cultures put their children down for the dark night, and then never respond to the cries of fear and loneliness. It is feared that to show tenderness, to reach out and console the fear and dislocation would spoil the child, make them too soft and unable to function in the world. But, how well do we really function anyway? We are a people consumed by the silenced cry, the agitation of our pain and the haunting of things little understood. We indulge the pain, ignore the pain or numb the pain, but we never understand its true source.

What did you see when you first looked into your parent's eyes? Did you gain a small taste of infinity submerged in the depths of your parent's love? Did you gain a first glimpse of who you really are reflected and magnified in the lens of their being? Or did you fall into the emptiness of their self-absorption and pain, the emptiness of being buried beneath their beliefs about life?

Do you fear the silence and the cry in its depths? Can you just sit silently in order to find the nature of the world below the cries of loneliness and fear?

Anadromous fish have held a fascination for cultures around the world. These are the fish that can pass from river to ocean and back again, can manage a life in both worlds. For the Pacific Coast these fish are primarily the salmon and steelhead, but also include stripped bass and shad. To the Yokuts, the steelhead was *tah-wah-aht* and the salmon was *ki-uh-khot*. The salmon and steelhead that entered the Golden Gate would pass through the northern reaches of the San Francisco Bay into the San Pablo Bay and then into the Carquinez Strait near my father's grave. From there the fish entered into the Sacramento/San Joaquin Delta. The delta marks the confluence of California's two great rivers that drain the Sierra/Cascade Range.

During the maddened frenzy of the Gold Rush the miners washed away entire mountainsides with giant hoses in their quest for gold. The hydraulic mining so filled the rivers with sediment that the delta could no longer be navigated and had to be dredged. An estimated 1.5 billion cubic yards of debris were washed out into the waterways that flowed into the delta, an amount of material sufficient to create a mile-wide highway a foot thick from San Diego to Seattle.

Once in the delta the fish turned north or south to seek out their home waters. Those turning south could choose an eastward turn to ascend the Sierra Nevada at the Mokelumne, the Tuolumne, the Stanislaus, the Merced, the Upper San Joaquin or the Kings.

The fish smell their home water. In one written account a

run of Chinook salmon were closed off from venturing to their home waters on the Upper San Joaquin because the rivercourse in between was dry. Game wardens tried to force them to go up the Merced toward Yosemite. Even when the fish were removed physically to the Merced they would swim back down to the San Joaquin. The fish just gathered at the weir that blocked their way and waited for a scent of their home water while the locals trapped, snagged and pitchforked them. The few that got through the weir ended up stranded in a shallow irrigation ditch. I wonder what went through the minds of the people as they participated in the destruction of a species? Did they tell these stories to their children with pride and wonder?

Migrants from Missouri and other parts of the south, called Pikes, populated much of the San Joaquin Valley of the nineteenth century. The Pikes were a rootless, dispossessed, landless people who had had no landscape to love, no landscape to form their greater mind, no history to understand. Awash in their pain and the silenced cry in their depths they squatted on the landscape of Valle de los Tulares and savagely claimed their rights to that land, their last chance at the edge of the continent, the last edge of the frontier. They dealt savagely with the Indians as well as with any other non-whites, whether Chinese or African-American or Mexican. They dealt savagely with all living things including themselves. They could get drunk on Saturday, go to church on Sunday morning, and then hunt Indians for sport on Sunday afternoon. Education wasn't necessary because the world was no larger than their pain. Their religion was no larger than their pain and fear. The Pike legacy still haunts the Great Valley, though the fish spirits still beckon, will always beckon.

The Chinook used to penetrate up the Kings River and also into Tulare Lake, if one can imagine forty-pound flashes of silver swimming in these places.

In mythology the salmon has come to represent Christ because of its ability to pass between the two worlds. In the story of the Fisher King a young prince was out wandering in the forest when he came upon a deserted camp. There was no one present but there was a salmon roasting on the spit. Being hungry and adventurous the boy reached out to take a piece of the fish for himself. The fish was so hot that it burned his hand. As he put his fingers into his mouth to cool them, a bit of the fish also fell into his mouth and he collapsed in agony. He lived in that agony for all but the last three days of his life. The only time he found peace was when he was fishing. He had had a sudden unexpected introduction to the other world and there had been no one there, no elder to guide him. He was alone, unschooled and unheard in his cries of agony.

There was a moment when I was about eleven or twelve when I looked all around me in this small town on the edge of the Great Valley and realized that no one really knew a thing about the true nature of life. Everyone was faking it as best they could and enduring life as best they could. I saw nothing but lives of quiet and not so quiet desperation. The fishing camp was empty, bereft of guides and teachers. There was no one who could answer my deeper questions let alone begin to contemplate them.

We attended a small fundamentalist church in Exeter. It stood across the street from some orange packing sheds that in turn stood by the railroad spur. The church was a wood sided building with white lap siding. In a gesture to modernity and an attempt to attract more worshippers a stucco front had been added. The rest of the structure remained the same, which gave the front a pasted-on quality.

It was always difficult for me to stay awake for the whole sermon. It took years for me to finally manage that feat. I remember sitting near the back and idly wondering who I really was as the sermon droned on. Who was this thing called John, this center of perception? Where did I really come from and what did I look like before I was born? It was a koan or Zen riddle asked of myself in ignorance. Suddenly I would sense emptiness and vastness. I found that I had no ground beneath my feet and I was filled with terror at losing who I was, even as painful as my life was, filled with terror at this insubstantial unreality. I had to fight to come home in my mind. This happened Sunday after Sunday and there was no one to talk to. The church was too fundamentalist to embrace the question and was too busy trying to convince me that just being alive was an act of sin. They were interested in nothing but the sound and repetition of their own story with little regard for stopping their narrative long enough to really see me or hear me. Their answer would have been to just read the Bible and to continue reciting the old story, a formula of little solace in my pain. My father could quote Biblical verses from memory with the best of them, but this rote knowledge never eased his pain. God never healed my sister and certainly never healed my father, despite my prayers. The church would have asked me to blindly and literally follow what I read in the holy book as the sole response to my sudden glimpse of seeing. I had been introduced to the other side. My life had no grounding and was so chaotic that I could not bear the terror of the question nor the terror of the answer. I desperately needed order. My grandfather helped provide what order he could in wordless fashion, but the answers were beyond him. My father's drunkenness may have been painful to me, but my greatest pain came from having no one to show me how to pass between the worlds. My world and I have been too small for the breadth and depth of seeing.

Even though my grandfather couldn't answer this riddle I loved him greatly. We worked in the fields together from when I was a child till I left for college, tending the grapes and peaches and plums. A young peach tree was his canvas and pruning shears his brush. He was a deacon in this church. I remember crawling on my knees with him gathering and husking walnuts, our hands stained brown. He told a joke and laughed in the middle of it, then said, "Shit." As a small child I was shocked at the earthiness and it changed my world. He had a great integrity, which I hope I learned well, but he couldn't save me from the hell in which I lived. I knew that he couldn't explain my trips to the void or save me from my father's house. No one had taught him and he didn't know the way himself. He was an illegitimate son of a Portuguese man in the midst of a German family, a dark secret unto himself. His mother and grandmother raised him, with old Dutch Bill himself a drunken presence. I somehow learned, though, while working those fields with him that the hills and the Sierra that loomed beyond them would always be there for me, be there like his memory in my mind.

In high school I had won all of the awards they gave for mathematics and science. But, despite my best efforts, the universities of my choice did not accept me. I ended up without enthusiasm at a school that was an afterthought, just to escape from my father who had never wanted his sons to go to college anyway. I started school as a Chemistry major. In high school, chemistry had been easy and the atoms had been presented rather simplistically and orderly. In college I encountered quantum theory and the Heisenberg Uncertainty Principle. It seemed that nothing could be known for sure and that I could never know if something was really in its proper place. Reality threatened to disappear into a blur of uncertainty and chaotic probability. The uncertainty, the chaos was too much for my mind and its need for order and structure. I changed majors because my mind was so overloaded that I couldn't process any more. I felt as I had before, sitting in the back of that church with the false stucco front. And still there was no one to talk to. Scientific theory was of little solace in the face of the human need for love and guidance, for seeing and being seen in the land of the blind.

The trouble with scientific theory is that it is not a vibrant story that engages our senses and penetrates to the depths of our beings. Our myths are our interface with the other world. They are the face that can be given to that which has no face.

We have forgotten our symbolic life and sheer literalism will be the death of the world. Literal fundamentalism exists in a mind gone rigid with fear. No wild birds with their gifts live in the world of literalism. We buy tame shadows of birds in the marketplace. Mythological symbols are the images that bridge the worlds like coursing, migrating Chinook. In the end we live and die, are enlightened or cursed by the symbols and images in our stories. Formulas are just formulas. What stories do we tell and what characters inhabit them?

I am walking in Exeter along F Street toward where it curves and heads northward out of town, in the direction of the old farm. As I pass the city limits I notice that the landscape has all reverted to its original wild state, with the earth rolling in hillocks covered with native grassland and scattered rock. A smile moves across my face and I feel a moment of joy. I step out into the wilderness and head north.

Chahkah Shahnau

Is your mind abundant? How has it come to its present state of being? Is it full of the nuance and fluidity of life or is it rigid and barren, painful and lonely? It is never too late to come back to the fullness of who you really are, to come back to knowing. Are you willing to restore the abundant landscape of your mind, maybe restory it? Is there an original story, one without words, only just knowing? Put another log on the fire if you wish to go further into all this. You need to stoke the fire a little for yourself.

Tulare Lake was once the largest fresh water lake west of the Mississippi and the area abounded in game. An account from 1850 told of "bands of elk, deer and antelope in such numbers that they actually darkened the plains for miles and looked in the distance like great herds of cattle." Commercial fisherman netted perch, mackerel and lake trout in great quantities. Ducks, geese, snipe and curlew thrived in the tules. Tulare Lake terrapin soup was on the menus of hotels up and down the West Coast. In 1852 Congress passed the Swamp and Overflowed Lands Act. The new land speculators and corporate farmers began to pump the lake bone dry to claim their wealth. It was as if a giant eraser now moved across the face of the map of the great Valle de los Tulares and suddenly it was all gone except for alkali and corporate farms. The land needed to be reclaimed from the forces that had created its abundance.

In December 1945, two years before I was born, Governor Earl Warren called the California Water Conference to session. He told those in attendance the following: "In my opinion we should not relax until California has adopted and put into operation a statewide program that will put every drop of water to work." What he was saying in effect was that if a drop of water made it to the sea, that it was a wasted drop. He didn't understand the spiritual dimensions of his economic vision. One speaker proposed that every river should be dammed and that the San Francisco Bay should be made into a freshwater lake. Due in part to these efforts the Friant Dam was completed on the upper San Joaquin in 1948. Soon there was no longer a spring run of Chinook because of the lack of water. The Bureau of Reclamation refused to release enough of their newly hoarded water for the fish to survive. To them it was a waste of water and effort and time. Those fish that attempted to make it through the shallow narrow sloughs made bow waves with their passage. These fish also became easy prey for the spear and pitchfork wielding folk along the waterways.

These folk appear to me as creatures from the *Night of the Living Dead*, their eyes glazed with some indescribable inner pain as they seek out the bright and the living. Like a bad dream in a bad movie their faces press to the lens and further distort the pain of their being. But, the Living Dead not only wielded the pitchforks, they also designed and built the dams, drained the vastness of the lake. They legislate our reality.

Once, years ago, as I passed through downtown Exeter I felt like crying at the state of my hometown. The town looked like a sad, decrepit near-corpse. The merchants of Visalia are always sucking the merchandising life out of the surrounding small towns, so there were a lot of empty stores, and a fire had burned down one of the old historic buildings at the exact center of town. The people responded by making a small park where the building once stood and then they broke out the paint. They painted murals all over downtown with pictures of their history. Exeter suddenly became more festive and the energy changed as the townsfolk changed their landscape in order to change the quality of their minds. There is much to be learned from this.

As you leave Exeter, moving toward the east, the road follows a right-angle grid through the orchards and groves, a Cartesian system laid out over the valley floor to create a form of order. The roads follow unseen section and half-section lines in homage to Rene Descartes. He is famous for his intellectual proof of the existence of God that began, "I think, therefore I am." But god I know that's not really true. Thinking is not necessarily knowing. Many of my thoughts have ripped me into pieces, speared me and left me thrashing on some rocky shore unable to really be.

Descartes is reputed to have been lying in bed one day observing the path of a fly as it crawled across the ceiling. He suddenly realized that he could communicate the position of that fly at any point in time by giving only two numbers. He had mentally overlaid a grid of lines on the ceiling and had only to give a left-right number and an up-down number, like latitude and longitude. He had established a mathematics of organization and predictability. The grid of roads suffices in the valley flatness but falls apart as soon as you begin to ascend *Chahkah Shahnau*, "Rocky Hill." The road is forced to curve around the flank of the hill before it reaches the crest. At the foot of the hill before its climb the road crosses the concrete lined V-channel of the Friant-Kern Canal that conducts its payload of water south from Friant Dam to waiting agribusiness. I read that an entomologist turned pesticide salesman in Fresno coined the word agribusiness. As the author noted, the word manages to take the culture out of agriculture.

During the summer the narrow blacktopped road up Chahkah Shahnau is lined with clumps of some kind of wild sunflower interspersed with dry dead thistle. I have cycled to the top and smelled the wild pungent chlorophyll smell of the sunflowers on a hot dry day. At the road's crest the valley is spread out below. The road at the top is lined with boulders, most of them covered with graffiti and surrounded by empty beer cans, cardboard six packs and brown paper bags. From here you can begin to see if you want to, but many come here just to further dull their senses.

To the north a gated and locked utility road leads up to the exclusive enclave of Badger Hill on Hawshau Shido. To the south rises the actual peak of Chahkah Shahnau, covered with rock formations and live oak, now topped with a microwave relay tower. I remember as a young Boy Scout hiking up among the rocks and discovering the pictographs painted there. I wonder if the paintings are still there or whether they are now defaced. Why is it that the pictographs seem to fit and be part of the landscape while the graffiti seems so jarring and out of place. These rocks along the roadway echo with some great emptiness behind their spray-painted markings. They echo with an isolation and pain, with the desperate scribbling of, "I am, I am, goddammit I am. I spray, therefore I am." The scattered cans and bottles seem left as mute testimony to these attempts at killing the pain. Maybe they are also left as a marker, a plea for someone or something to notice and extend a hand, for the fish spirit to ascend even to this summer dry place.

Looking out across the valley the vast checkerboard grid is made obvious. In the foreground the Friant-Kern Canal slices across the landscape. The first settlers here settled in the fertile delta land of the Kaweah and its streams. The thick groves of oaks provided food, firewood and shade from the hot sun. Acorns were a commercial crop for years. A well was only a shallow hole in the sand. The area here below Chahkah Shahnau was originally dry rolling hog-wallows that undulated across the landscape and not settled till much later. All of that has fallen to the landplane, everything leveled and squared off. Old Dutch Bill was the first to grow grain in the region in 1869. He scattered wheat seed over a 160-acre plot and plowed it under with a crew using single plows. In this area away from the river delta everything had to be dry farmed, this in a place where it never rained from spring till late autumn. In 1872 the railroad came through the valley and the grain business began to take off, the land around Exeter began to be leveled in earnest, a victim of the Fresno scraper.

The order of things there below is obvious. While growing up I needed the comfort and obviousness of the valley's order because I was surrounded by more chaos and unpredictability than I could bear. I had to have something that I could hold on to. Somewhere I needed something outside myself that I could rely on, something that I could count on to be exactly where it should be at any given moment. People certainly never had been. While taking those college chemistry classes and dealing with Heisenberg I remember putting in late night chem labs accompanied by gnawing pains in my stomach that wouldn't go away. The next summer I was home trying to sleep one night. My mind began to fall into a great spiral of ever increasing blackness, fear and terror that sucked me down. I made it into the bathroom where I fell into the black spiral once again. My father heard me fall, then picked me up like a baby. He was 6'2" and 240 pounds. I awoke in his arms. It was the only time I can remember that he ever held me. I had a bleeding ulcer, a hole burned into my gut as with a laser.

I once met a Choctaw medicine man many years later. He took one look at me and said, "It looks like the Energy has been beating you up." By Energy he meant the life force that emanates from the other side. The Chinese call it "chi," the Japanese call it "ki." The Hindus call it "prana." It is the Salmon Energy of the infinite. My life was rife with this unguided coursing Energy that battered my daily life. I thought about this for a while and about my father. Months later I saw the medicine man and said, "I've been thinking. Way down deep my father was a sensitive man. I bet the Energy beat him up so badly that he drank to kill the pain. I bet most drunks do." The medicine man looked at me and smiled. "If you were to round up all of the winos in L.A. and wire them together, you could blow up the whole goddamn town."

Now, in the old days, if you gazed across the valley from

here atop Chahkah Shahnau you might have seen the ninety-mile silver glint of Tulare Lake as the sun set behind the coastal mountains. The Kaweah flowed into the meanders of the delta and the many meanders flowed into the lake. In the old dry lakebed the meandering streams are now ditches and canals that move in straight lines and then abruptly move at right angles at a section line, all carefully laid out and managed. The canals both irrigate and drain the fields. The drainage water is laced with heavy metals like arsenic and selenium that collect in reservoirs where the vestigial flocks of waterfowl gather and try to successfully reproduce despite the twisting of their genes. The land of the once fecund lake bottom is now itself so deformed that I always want to hurry past and avert my eyes in shame, pray for a bit of forgiveness. In places, the hard thick layer of leached salts on the surface of the ground looks like a covering of ice or snow.

It seems that we seek the obvious with little patience for the unobvious. The unobvious is only that because of lack of patience and because of a lack of courage to explore beyond the obvious. Mathematicians have now moved on from the strict linear order of Descartes to chaos theory, or non-linear dynamics. In the midst of some seeming spiraling chaos can be found the seeds of some non-ordinary ordering principle, but maybe we prefer the ease of a seedless reality. In our minds we pull back from the perception of chaos as being the work of the devil and in so doing usually do the work of the devil as we try to subjugate reality into a concrete-lined, predictable form. We are not willing to wait long enough, to just watch and see. The shortest distance between two points may not be a straight line, there can be an unfamiliar, unknown certainty at the core of uncertainty and true control may come about without force.

When I gaze out across the valley I know that you can begin to see if you want to. When I'm here and a breeze stirs carrying the untamed rank smell of the sunflowers, it brings me back to earth and stone, live oak and dried thistle. To the east is the Yokohl Valley where the family originally settled. When I look in that direction something quickens in my spirit. Looking further east the jagged peaks rise tumultuously. I am aware of all this and its reflection in my mind. I am aware of being aware of all this, therefore for this moment I am. I simply choose to be aware. I simply choose to be able to divine something deeper. I am now drawn to crags, meanders and uncertainty even as I raise a family. There is more to be learned beyond this Cartesian farm belt, eastward where the Sierra beckon.

Coyote Genesis

What does it mean to have ground beneath your feet, a ground that can catch your footsteps no matter what realm you explore? Can there be such a thing, have you experienced such a thing?

This kind of ground resides in mind and memory, the memory of being welcomed and loved into being and of the shaping of neural circuits that are nurtured and pruned by loving hands. This ground travels everywhere beneath the feet, in all realities. The road can be traveled without this magic carpet of remembered welcome, but it is harder, much harder. I know this.

Why did your parents call you into this world? Can you face this question? Were you labor for their farm, support for their old age, a replacement, a patch for their marriage, a maternal urgent need, a burden, another conscript for their religion? What would it mean to be really welcomed into this great house for who you truly are?

What legacy will you leave your children? Will they be able to move freely between the worlds without fear, stepping forward on the ground of love that you have spread beneath their feet, thinking clearly and freely in a well-tended great mind?

Or will they be part of the Living Dead?

Weep, weep. Face your emptiness to know the fullness of being, let the fire warm you. Welcome to here. Welcome.

Descending the backside of Chahkah Shahnau the narrow road is lined with barbed wire fences and several varieties of wildflowers that can sustain themselves in summer dryness. At the bottom of the valley a ribbon of green grasses follows the valley fold where water seeps to the surface from underground. During the winter and spring this is the watercourse for Yokohl Creek. The green is in stark contrast to the yellow dry grass of summer days. The dried grasses cover the rest of the landscape; yellow hills roll toward the Sierra. Cattle scatter here and there, the mud churned and cut by their hooves. The road reaches a T intersection at the bottom. To the right is the Yokohl Valley, which provides a back door to the old family land. To the left is a return to the Mineral King Highway along the backside of Hawshau Shido. This is where the Sierra foothills begin their uplift in earnest.

This area begins what I call Coyote's landscape. In the primal times here, there were four main predators apart from man. They were grizzly bear, wolf, mountain lion and coyote. Grizzly bear and wolf have been eliminated though grizzly bear still ironically appears on our state flag. Lion keeps to its secretive ways. I know that I am being watched but I don't quite know from where. Coyote just keeps on keeping on through guile and perseverance. We're never quite able to put our finger on him. Coyote of course is the trickster of Native American myth along with Crow. Ethnologists have always been trying to pin him down. He is this thing, but no, he's that. Coyote is the Heisenberg Uncertainty Principle of the mind.

In the past I have had an uneasy relationship with Coyote. I found it difficult to maintain a close relationship with a God that can allow Coyote to exist in the infinite wisdom of things. Where in the realm of love is there justification for some scurrilous Coyote who would just as soon take your money and laugh and run as do anything else? How do you maintain a relationship with that? Where is love, compassion and kindness when Coyote is always lurking around?

I'll tell you what I do know of old Coyote. Coyote represents our own capacities for constant self-deception, and also represents God's attempt to shock us out of our stupor of predictability. As soon as I think that I know something fully, Coyote will quickly, unceremoniously let me know that I don't. If I am unawake, Coyote will steal me blind, but it is only because I am blind and asleep. He will always bite me in the ass if I am not aware. Always.

My daughter loves coyote stories. Maybe she can embrace these tales of raucous humor, trickery, uncertainty and deception because she is embraced in the certainty of her parents' love for her. I've written a few for her. Recently I watched a pair of coyotes out hunting in the early morning near a freeway, uncaring of the concrete reality, noses to the breeze, ears alert. I am also reminded of when I was teaching in the 1970s and taught High Sierra backpacking for summer school. We were camped on a ridge over a canyon, Lake Tahoe far below us in the distance. I rose before dawn to watch the lake come alive in the light. The ridgelines to the east were just silhouettes of dark, darker and black. Bats were darting everywhere in their last nocturnal sweeps. The light began to further separate the eastern ridges and gave them some color and texture.

The lake began to glow. Suddenly there was a coyote howl to the new sun and then other howls from other points in the echoing canyon. The howls were interspersed with the short yips of pups trying to learn this primal greeting to the day. I sat cold and hunkered, mesmerized by the scene. I felt a depth of sadness well up as I wondered when I'd be able to teach my own to howl, to sing. It took a lot of years.

Despite whatever desires we may have for an ordered and predictable reality, the earth is always moving beneath our feet. The pace may be imperceptible on a human scale, but the shreds of evidence are all around. The continents were once many, became one, then became many again in a different form and configuration. The lands and oceans changed size and shape, creating new climates, currents and temperatures, all the while bearing their load of protoplasm, of organisms that had to adapt to the metamorphosis of the land.

The continents came together to create the one great continent, Pangaea, and the world ocean, Panthalassa. Pangaea split north and south into Laurasia and Gondwana separated by the Tethys seaway. The equatorial current could now flow round the world. Currents changed, temperatures changed. The North American plate drifted westward as the different oceans formed until it encountered the submerged Pacific plate and overrode it. North America, like a great bulldozer blade scraped up oceanic material before it and began to form mountains. Molten rock extruded and became a great granite slab that tilted upward until the great forces of creation were too much. The uplift snapped and settled, leaving great escarpments and canyons above a rift valley to the east, hundreds of miles long.

This was the creation of the Sierra Nevada. It has been scoured and carved by glaciers, shaken by earthquakes and lifted here and there by volcanoes. What little plant life that could take hold in the decomposing granite would die, compost, rise again, die and compost, slowly creating soil. Creeping, crawling, twittering, roaring life began to follow the plant life into higher and higher rocky places. Here in the southern Sierra the Sequoia Gigantea took hold.

Once when I was in my midtwenties I was riding around stoned out of my mind in the backseat of a large American automobile listening to loud rock and roll on the car stereo. Suddenly I pictured all of the ancestors that had come before me, all of the people and plants and animals, the stardust falling into suns and planets. And here I was, a glorified stoned monkey with a dulled mind cruising the dark streets in the backseat of that car blindly looking for some light. I was just another Living Dead. I knew that in the face of the power of countless eons of evolution that had created me in this moment that I had to live in more than a mindless stupor. We owe a certain dignity to the enormity of the things that have made us. In light of the great magnitude of existence, we need to decide to be more than just assholes and Living Dead for our seventy plus years of life.

When most people view the great process of evolution they see tumult, conflict and mere survival and use it to justify their greed, their violence. I can see the seeds in the apparent face of violent chaos, the deep underlying cooperation among all beings in moving toward consciousness and in choosing what to become.

Barbara and I are in a darkened room with another couple who seem dark and troubled. They offer us an easy way to make money. On the coffee table I see a brick of cocaine or what I take to be cocaine. It is some compressed white powder. I tell the man I could really appreciate the money but my experience has told me that if I were to sell drugs I would ingest too much myself and end up making no money anyway.

At this point something happens. I freeze and wake up in the daylight standing in the exact same place. It seems as if somehow these dark people have done this to me. I wonder how many cycles of nights and days that I have been frozen. As I leave to drive down the street I find myself aware that dealing drugs takes many forms in life and that I have been frozen for a great many cycles of nights and days, perhaps countless cycles.

Grand and cool swelled up the forest; sharp and rugged rose the wave of white peaks, their vast fields of snow rolling over the summit in broad shining masses.

Sunshine, exuberant vegetation, brilliant plant life, occupied our attention hour after hour until the middle of the second day. At last, after climbing a long, weary ascent, we rode out of the dazzling light of the foothills into a region of dense woodland, the road winding through avenues of pines so tall that the late evening light only came down to us in scattered rays.

... Our eyes often ranged upward, the long shafts leading the vision up to green, lighted spires, and on to the clouds. All that is dark and cool and grave in color, the beauty of umbrageous distance, all the sudden brilliance of strong local lights tinted upon green boughs of red and fluted shafts, surround us in ever-changing combination as we ride along these winding roadways of the Sierra.

We had marched a few hours over high, rolling wooded ridges, when in the late afternoon we reached the brow of an eminence and began to descend. Looking over of the tops of the trees beneath us we saw a mountain basin fifteen hundred feet deep surrounded by a rim of pine-covered hills. An even unbroken wood covered these sweeping slopes down to the very bottom, and in the midst, open to the sun, lay a circular green meadow, about a mile in diameter.

As we descended, side wood-tracks, marked by the deep ruts of timber wagons, joined our road on either side, and in the course of an hour we reached the basin and saw the distant roofs of Thomas's Saw-Mill Ranch. We crossed the level disk of the meadow, fording a clear, cold mountain stream, flowing, as the best brooks do, over clean white granite sand, and near the northern margin of the valley, upon a slight eminence, in the edge of a magnificent forest, pitched our camp.

—Clarence King

When I graduated from high school my impulse was to leave home as quickly as I could. The day after graduation I left to take a job on the maintenance crew at a YMCA camp in the Sierra. It was almost a hundred years to the day after King had set out on his exploration. The camp was near the old Thomas Saw-Mill Ranch. I remember on one of our days off that we all went hiking to a great meadow. We ate our lunches on the top of one of the stumps of the Sequoia grove that had grown for thousands of years in this place. The stumps were twelve to fifteen feet across and about four to six feet high. They had all been cut to feed the mill.

The *Sequoia gigantea* of the Sierra differs from its cousin, the coastal redwood (*Sequoia sempervirens*). All of the light-weight, flexible, strong redwood that we see in buildings and furniture comes from the coastal redwood. The Giant Sequoia in comparison is hard and brittle. It is so brittle that when it is felled, the tremendous weight combined with the height of the fall fractures the wood and leaves it useless for anything but two thousand year old fence posts. Two-thirds of the groves in the southern Sierra were cut.

The Giant Sequoia grows from the tiniest of seeds. The Giant Sequoia is a truly useless tree except for its beauty and grandeur, its gesture toward the greater immensity. Yet the groves were felled anyway. I've seen photographs of the loggers standing proudly before a downed Sequoia, bearded, heavy booted and grim like my own ancestors of that time, blind to the evidence all around them. They were blinded by the long hard days of work and the nights of log camp drinking, blinded by a pain that had dogged them since Eden. The bright and the living had been felled for no great reason, dragged down and splintered, then used to fence the earth into definable portions.

Things shift beneath the feet. What can be known for certain? The mountains begin here from Coyote's landscape and rise from the boulders and live oak to the granite domes and Giant Sequoias, but they don't endure. What are the seeds?

Coyote Genesis

Well, whatever it was,
maybe God,
flowed along for quite a while in a place
where there was no while or place, unknowable
and unknowing. Then suddenly
creation happened,
the ten thousand things happened,
and whatever it was found a voice
and said, "This is good," and I think
that whatever it was
meant it. But,
there was a problem with this paradise—
a little boring
maybe, too slow, you know how nothing
changes in a sleepy little town—
and whatever it was had bigger fish to fry.
There were these two newcomers,
but they were as slow as anyone or
anything else,
with one difference: they could be tempted, or
rather, should I say, tricked.
So whatever it was became a brown coyote,
stopped for a moment to appreciate his form reflected
in a nearby puddle,
farted twice,
licked his balls, then told the newcomers,

"Don't eat that fruit," and trotted off.
Coyote then found himself taken
by the sight of his own penis, decided
to revel in that one for a moment, and so
became a snake,
an emerald green tree snake, or maybe
it was just his penis painted day-glo and hung
around the tree like an arrow,
pointing at what was forbidden.
The snake said, "Eat it. Who you gonna believe:
me or that hairy coyote god who
licks his balls?"
Well, who were they gonna believe: a glistening
emerald green talking tree snake or a
flatulent brown coyote?
Choices, choices,
suddenly there were choices, like
an eight–alarm fire bell in a sleepy little town.
Creation heated up;
the ten thousand things heated up.
Coyote mocked the newcomers from his hiding place,
thundered and damned a little to keep
things interesting while they hung their heads,
convinced that they'd chosen the prize
from behind the wrong door.
They passed this story on to their kids,
while coyote laughed from
behind the tree.

The Fool

It seems strange that you must spend the night here in order to awaken. It is never easy. Once awake, though, it is best to not go back to sleep. You can try if you want, but you can never quite go back to sleep again. Because of this the pain is much worse if you try to ignore knowing. Much worse.

How did you feel when you heard the story of how Coyote created the world? Did you laugh? Were you shocked and offended? Was there something dark and objectionable that you didn't want to penetrate? Coyote hits us with a stick. Thwack! Go below your beliefs and see what is. Go below your objections and see what is. Just sit, just go. It's too late to turn away. Who are you below what others have told you to think and believe? There is something valuable that exists below gossip and comparisons, below fear and greed. What is the nature of that gold?

Imagine catching a momentary glimpse of a gleam of that gold in the darkness. Suddenly you laugh because it's all so clear and then you cry at what we've done with the gift. Tears and laughter, tears and laughter, then it's gone.

Which is worse, the pain of awakening or the pain of the great emptiness that pulls at the edges of your being, the pain that you try to hide in the dark unseen corners of your mind?

Let me tell you of the Buddha, the Awakened One: his life was far different than mine, and probably yours, born a prince in a royal family in India. His father chose to keep him sheltered from the misery of the world, of the losses of aging and the reality of dying. When he was twenty-nine the Buddha spied a decrepit old man stumbling along the road. The old man had made it through the king's guards who always swept the prince's route to keep out the dark and objectionable. The Buddha's world was shaken. The next day the Buddha spied a man sick and decrepit lying in his own shit along the roadway. On the third day the Buddha caught his first sight of death, a body readied for the pyre. He looked at his own flesh in horror, seeing for the first time that it too was destined to rot and decay, a thing suddenly become vile, a "bag of excrement and bones." Old age, sickness and dying were dramatically thrust into his reality.

On the fourth day the Buddha spied a monk along the road and made his choice to leave all he knew. On the same day, his son was born. On hearing the news, the Buddha called him *Rahula*, meaning "impediment," and that became his son's name. The Buddha then left all behind, even his son and his wife, to begin his search.

But I have to stop this story right here—to tell you that I am certainly no Buddha, wouldn't desire to be, because I longed for and searched for a family a very long time. My daughter is no impediment; rather my love for her has enlightened me. My grandparents' bodies rot in their graves, their farm gone to rubbish and dust, yet their memory helps guide me through this night. The Buddha's search was guided and colored by his repulsion at old age, decay and dying. I was raised amidst the disgraces of life and yet have touched some grace. Listen to me, stop wherever you are and go through the door of your circumstances. Renouncing the world divides the world, cuts it into more fragments and pieces, and divides it into the holy and the unholy. Step through the door where you are and begin to put things back together.

What are your circumstances, what brought you to this fire to sit with me, to listen to my stories? Why would you want to spend time here? Yes, sleep is seductive. It's a long night and it seems it would be so easy to go back to sleep, back to the numbness of not knowing.

Yet even in the midst of sleep have you awakened within your dreams, pierced the nature of that world?

I look around in the dream and find myself back on a construction site. Another carpenter hands me a magic mushroom, dipped and preserved in honey. I'm afraid to eat it. I'm afraid of seeing too much, of not being able to cope in the world after eating it. As I awaken I am totally unable to recall where I am or who I am. I am just awareness. I keep asking myself where am I, who am I, what am I?

A Carpenter's Lunchbreak

We all sit down for lunch, some
passing a joint, and the newspaper is spread at my feet,
telling the story of an imprisoned IRA

hunger striker now dead
and a day-by-day account for the vicarious sort
of what it's like, slowly losing the senses
as death creeps through.
I'm reminded of my friend Jayram
and tell everyone of this man from my
ashram days,
who so hungered for God
that he fasted to see him.
Jayram was near six feet tall, died weighing eighty pounds,
purple viscera
showing through his pale translucent skin.
Hoarse and gravel voiced ex-con Bob
allows as how he'd fasted once while doing hard time
and at the end of some fourteen days
took LSD,
smuggled in as painted colored heads
in some Alice in Wonderland scene.
"Some trip," he rasps and laughs
as I shiver,
picturing a mind suddenly too large for words
in some small cell behind cold grey walls.

I need to tell you more about the Fisher King and his salmon dreams. The Fisher King now presides over the Grail Castle where every night a procession of beauty files by that he can only watch, but cannot experience. A maiden carries the lance that pierced the side of Christ, another the paten that held the bread at the Last Supper. Finally another maiden carries the Grail Cup that carried the wine, the blood of the Christ spirit, the life giving essence, healer and fulfiller of all who drink of it. The King can only watch in dull agony, untouched by beauty, unable to drink of the Grail. He can witness the fullness of life but never taste it. In this state of being he is only King of the Living Dead, a too large mind viewing the world from within his small grey cell.

An old man once told me a story. He said that I reminded him of Parsifal. Now the name Parsifal means "innocent fool." I don't know if I have always been innocent, but I've certainly been a fool. The name also means "he who draws the opposites together." It means that somehow this fool of a boy has to be able to meet old Coyote, look him in the eye, find some sustaining ground beneath his feet and not flinch in the mangy face of loss, of chaos and contradiction.

So as the story goes, Parsifal was born in Wales (my grandmother was part Welsh), a rube on the fringe of civilization. He didn't know it yet, but in his quest he would have to somehow heal the Fisher King, to redeem him from living death. Parsifal had no father, no knowledge of his roots, no history. He was just a boy who lived on a small piece of land in the middle of nowhere and did what he did to help with survival.

Imagine how it would seem when one day the larger world intruded and five knights came riding past the farmhouse, then left. They were like riders from another world. Parsifal was entranced and astounded. Maybe they could help answer some of the questions. Who am I really, where did I come from, what should I do? Maybe they could point him to something, something he could find, something that he could attain that would fill the emptiness, ease the loneliness of being so isolated and small.

I wonder if, as Parsifal left home and entered the unknown forest, ravens didn't circle overhead mocking and encouraging in the same swoop of sound. Gaw! Gaw! Fool!

Fool! Red Kaweah, Black Kaweah, Kaweah Queen. It's only rocks, it's only ice. You're only a sinner, a small bag of bones and shit locked in a small grey cell. Look it in the eye.

Clarence King was on such a quest. When King and his party left the camp at Thomas's Saw-Mill Ranch they descended into Kings River Canyon. Some believe that the Kings River was named for him, but it wasn't. It's real name is Rio de los Santos Reyes, the River of the Holy Kings, because it was discovered on January 6, the Day of Epiphany, the day the Magi arrived to meet the Christ child. The party turned south at Roaring River and ascended a long smooth glacial moraine ridge. From there they ascended to the top of Mt. Brewer, a peak that he named for one of his companions. What they saw staggered them, because there was yet another range of even higher peaks to the east. These were the peaks that King had seen from the top of Mt. Bullion above the Mariposa goldfields. The view above timberline was one of vast granite reaches punctuated by the blue discs of frozen and half frozen lakes, the blues at once eerie, cold and enticing. Sheer walls plummeted downward thousands of feet and formed granite walled canyons that broke the high vast expanse.

King had reserved the name Whitney for the highest peak and he knew that he had to get there. Being the first to summit the highest point in California, and perhaps the entire country, had become his grail. King had calculated that the mountain lay somewhere near the head of the Kings and Kaweah rivers.

The mountains in this region of the Sierra form two parallel north-south ranges with a great canyon between. A range of peaks crosses this chasm from east to west to separate the waters of the Kings and the Kern. Mt. Brewer anchors the northern end of the Great Western Divide. A little south of Mt. Brewer the Kings-Kern Divide intersects the Great Western Divide. Ski mountaineers call this the Sierra High Route and use it to cross the mountains in midwinter, never descending below ten thousand feet.

King and his climbing partner had to descend the sheer side of Mt. Brewer and then ascend the steep flank of the Kings-Kern Divide into another realm of ice and cold. The ridge is narrow and then falls steeply away to the south. They descended by rope, constantly flicking it from each belay point above, cutting off any chance of going back in that direction. From the Kern Canyon they ascended to the top of a mountain that King called Mt. Tyndall.

At the top of Mt. Tyndall they could look back on the granite and ice reaches they had just traversed. To the east was the chalky, mysterious lunar range of the White Mountains, home to bristlecones that were millennia old even when Christ was born. To the south six miles away was the granite dome of Whitney, close, yet out of reach of their food supplies and battered bodies. They could not continue.

What do you see in the coyote face of the chaotic unknown? Can you penetrate it? You can't reach for a rulebook to govern your frontier, there is none. You must map the vast reaches of your own mind. There is only seeing, one eye on the polestar and the greater cosmos, the other on the place where your foot falls next.

Dumtah

Have you ever had a vision, a glimpse of understanding or beauty that momentarily stopped your life? You may have had the vision and cannot remember. Fear is a great eraser. Something always struggles to come forth through the fear, struggles with being draped in the fear, and having to wear a mask of the fear.

Mind

Black flag-tailed lynx on a rockstrewn hillside
arching through spring grasses
like a porpoise through deep green waves.
With a bound and another bound
its claws extend suddenly these 50 yards
shredding the curtain between
this and that.
Ah the sunlit grass covered convolutions of this mind
a silent blacktailed thought running through.

After six years of searching, the Buddha sat beneath the Bodhi tree and attained his great understanding. He then went on to teach. He declared that there are Four Noble Truths, the first of which is the truth of suffering, that the nature of life is suffering.

I'll tell you truthfully, I have a different understanding. The nature of life is that it is. A dog feels pain yet does not suffer. Suffering is the belief that the pain is life itself and will always be. Suffering is the fear that life is only this. Suffering is largely a human conceit, a human perception.

The first noble truth is this. Fear exists. It permeates all that we see, do and think. We fear life because we think it is suffering, we fear life because we think it is sin or we think it an illusion to rise above. We simply fear the great act of being alive and the attendant risk of exercising our minds. We create all manner of rationalizations for our fear and for our being here. There are the Four Noble Truths, the Eight Fold Path, the Ten Commandments, life sanctified by whole numbers, life by the numbers. These are the great summings up, life in a nutshell. What if I told you that the number of Noble Truths is an irrational number? We are always willing to have someone or something tell us what to do or think rather than risk real knowing.

As the Buddha traveled around India he invited his devotees to come join him and live the wandering existence. He declared it a quicker path to enlightenment than staying in the world. As the Buddha and his followers traveled they would stop in the villages and collect their alms, their means of existence, from those who were left behind in ignorance. It was a form of spiritual capitalism, to divide the world and live off the other half.

But what is life really? Sense your breath of atoms. Sense the ground beneath your feet, the innumerable stars over your head. They spring from the silent core of seeming chaos, vibrating in nothingness. You have to go there for yourself, no matter where you are.

Accept disgrace willingly.
accept misfortune as the human condition.
What do you mean by "Accept disgrace willingly"?
Accept being unimportant.
Do not be concerned with loss or gain.
This is called "Accepting disgrace willingly."
What do you mean by "Accept misfortune as the human
    condition"?
Misfortune comes from having a body.
Without a body, how could there be misfortune?
Surrender yourself humbly; then you can be
    trusted to care for all things.
Love the world as your own self; then you can truly
    care for all things.

—Lao Tsu

Ching Man Ching in his treatise on T'ai Chi Chuan coun-sels, "Learn to invest in loss. Who is willing to do this? To invest in loss is to permit others to attack while you don't use even the slightest force to defend yourself. On the contrary, you lead the opponent's force away so that it is useless. Then when you counter, any opponent will be thrown out a great distance."

What a difficult concept this has been to accept. Much of my life has seemed to be wrapped up in such loss. Jesus said, "Turn the other cheek," but I have misunderstood. In the mar-tial arts that I study, one turns a cheek and also steps aside from the attack. As I grew up I learned only to try and hold my place directly in the path of the great forces at hand. Either that, or run away. For me, too often in the past, loss has meant being left rigid, bloodied and broken from resistance or being left in flight and fear. So I greatly resisted understanding loss, because I had never known its real teaching. Investing in loss is the third way, the unknown way.

I once had a vision where all the people of the world were within my field of view. They were laid out as in a colorful tapestry or rich neural network. There was movement everywhere and as one person encountered another, that encounter determined the next. A person could always choose a direction at each encounter. A person was never so far from God, so far from the Great Spirit, that they couldn't change their mind by changing the nature of the encounter at hand. The paths stretched behind everyone like vapor trails and as these trails touched and interwove, the tapestry came into being, came to life. It had the bright color and weave of Mayan cloth. As I watched, a voice said, "Pain is only the resistance to the learning." I opened my eyes and I was crying.

But since then I have still felt so much pain. Why should this be so? Why had my life not been suffused with bliss? It was only a vision and vision alone doesn't make a life, doesn't walk on human legs, doesn't walk the road. Vision alone is cheap, is clever and meaningless. I was being counseled, "Learn to invest in loss. Don't hold fast to your fixed position, your fixed beliefs. Change your mind, change your life." The vision has had to be eaten and digested, taken into the heart and bone marrow. It is the Coyote Teaching, "Learn to invest in loss."

As the Mineral King Highway enters the tiny area of Lindcove, Mehrten Drive turns off to both the north and south. To the north is an old two-story wooden house that used to belong to my Uncle Will. Really he was my great-great uncle Will. He was Dutch Bill's son. That house seemed to be a labyrinth of mysteries to me as a child, when we would all gather for reunions and Uncle Will would preside as patriarch. If you turn south on Mehrten Drive you head toward Dumtah. As you drive down the narrow blacktopped road you can see the homes on five-acre parcels that have sprung up in recent years as the ranch has had to be subdivided. This all was part of the Mehrten brother's holdings in the nineteenth century as they owned or controlled thirty thousand acres of these hills and valleys. In the Panic of 1893 they lost most all of this land, foreclosed on by the Bank of Italy for the sum of twenty thousand dollars. Family stories still echo with images of shyster lawyers and dubious dealings. In the feeding frenzy that followed the foreclosure, the land was divided among developers all out to make the fastest buck possible.

The land on both sides of this road was divided into five- and ten-acre lots advertised as Lindcove Villa. Even in the 1890s the prospect of planting orange groves was a lure. Brochures and advertisements were distributed in Southern California and on the East Coast touting the possibilities for citrus ranches. Tours were conducted and special trains made their runs. A plot of orange trees was planted, but they froze in the winter and died in the summer's drought. When large groups of potential buyers were supposed to make their tour up Mehrten Avenue what they saw were large sucker limbs broken off citrus trees that had grown somewhere else. They had been stuck in the ground to look like an orchard. Old Dutch Bill's descendents managed to reacquire most of the subdivided lots but now it is subdivided again, the IRS and inheritance taxes forcing a finish to what the Bank of Italy had started.

Old Dutch Bill was no stranger to sorrow and loss. In 1892

his partner/brother Louis had been killed in San Francisco under mysterious circumstances, maybe murder. In the previous five years Bill had lost five children, two sets of newborn twins and a seven-year-old daughter, Kate. Kate had been in a buggy accident and seemed to be recovering when she was somehow given the wrong medicine, causing her death. On the heels of all this loss, he then lost his physical world to the Bank of Italy. He began to drink heavily.

I can feel old Dutch Bill's sorrow even now. It is in my being, a weight around my spirit. It is an old tale in this family whispered by circling crows. My mother never knew these stories growing up, but somehow heard the whispering crows and took it to heart, the same drama reenacted sixty years later in our lives. There was my sister Susan, my parents' near bankruptcy and crushing debt, and of course my father's ensuing drunken binges.

It's said that Dutch Bill would go to Visalia to borrow money to pay his ranch hands, but before he left town he'd get drunk and get rolled once more, then have to borrow money again. In December 1897 he and his sons camped between Visalia and Tulare where they were raising their hogs on acorns beneath a great stand of valley oaks. He took the train to Visalia looking for additional money but everyone turned him down. Somebody stopped to entertain him with more drink, a chance to drown the sorrow and loss. He got back on the train for Tulare. The conductor was going to let him off at the hog ranch beneath the oaks, but old Bill was too drunk and too helpless. The conductor took him on to Tulare where he was laid on a baggage truck, then taken to jail. The officer making his rounds found Bill dead in his cell.

Despite his near pauper status, old Dutch Bill was still a prominent man. Nobody wanted any responsibility for his death and the county judge and the coroner wanted it all to go away. There was a quick funeral and burial. Family stories say there is really no one in Dutch Bill's grave, that the officials came and took his body from the family graveyard after burial so we would have nothing on which to base further claims. All of the great effort of immigration, the family dividing in New York, some coming overland, some around the Horn, all of this effort culminating in drunken loss. My grandfather was a teetotaler in response. Loss piled upon loss. Mehrten loss piled upon Spivey loss, an inheritance of loss. Body or no body, I know that he's still about. The crows tell me that. They also tell me that I have to find him and lay him to rest with the great family.

As you wind through the granite and oak covered hills, the blacktopped road becomes dirt. At the transition is a gate, where I've watched coveys of quail scurry through the dry yellow grass. It's a bit further to Dumtah. What is Dumtah? Today there are probably few people that know of this place deep in Mehrten Valley. Dumtah Flat is the site of a large year-round spring, a place where the Indians always found water and had a village. The area is surrounded with oaks bearing their loads of acorns, the Yokuts' primary food source. Many of the Yokuts and Paiute tribes used the area, the Wachumne, the Yokodo, the Gaweah, the Pahdwishe. This is also where the Mehrten family first settled and built their homestead. The surrounding area is full of great flat rocks pockmarked with mortar holes where the Yokuts ground the acorn into flour. There is a great sense of awe and mystery for me about this place, as if this is the birthplace of my world as I know it. This is where our family first entered this landscape, our *sipapu*. It is where we first emerged into this new world. It as if the earth gave birth to us here, and the spring brought us forth in the water of a new life, into a new mystery. This is our Eden.

How did my family look on all of those Yokuts that had preceded them here? Did they call them "Diggers" like other settlers did? "Diggers," the name that John Fremont had pinned on any of the Indians living here in California, named that in derision for living off pine nuts and acorns. It was as if the Indians smelled of barbarism in a progressive time of gunpowder and gold. How did the Indians view these newcomers, these invaders? In 1870 the family apprehensively watched many of the Indians file by on their way to the great Ghost Dance, the *Heut Hetwe*, in Eshom Valley. Eshom Valley, *Chetutu* or Clover Place. Some even came to the door for handouts. The family watched the Yokuts and other tribes file along the dirt trail, through the outcroppings of granite, wind along the creek bottoms and over the dry leaves, fallen acorns and galls beneath the old oak trees. What nervousness and fear the family must have felt as they watched the Yokuts go to this last gasp appeal to the Great Spirit, like asking for clemency or a stay of execution. "Why have these misfortunes overcome us?"

The Yokuts danced their appeal to *Tih-pik-nits*, the bird person who was the keeper of the hereafter. Tih-pik-nits would bring back all of the ancestors, the relatives, the fathers, the mothers, uncles and aunts and grandparents. No one would have to die anymore. Life in all its sacredness would be restored. The dance was to last for six days. After five days the settlers, fearing for their lives, broke it up.

Not far away are the remains of *arrastras* built by the Spanish. These are large horse-powered mill stones used to grind gold ore. They were there long before the family, mysteries even to them. How much gold had there been and who had dug it? No one has ever answered those questions. Also nearby are the remains of old pictographs, their meaning unknown. When I was last in this place I could hear crows call from one of the oak trees and for a moment I thought I saw Coyote laughing from behind the great trunk. What else had come forth from that spring? What energies unleashed unknowingly into this family from this land? I hear the voices of those who have gone before. Kaweah, Kaweah. Red Kaweah, Black Kaweah, Kaweah Queen. Their spirits seem to enter me from the soles of my feet where I meet the ground. Had my family been so penetrated, had they heard the murmurs in this place, the message of the crow people and the howl of Coyote? How did their ordered German minds meet the chaos of this great unknown, the upwellings of Energy not understood? I think that I see faces and they ask for a voice. I am of this place and this land.

*I am in a desert setting with an old grey, male
shaman. It feels like somewhere south of the border
and we are both sitting on the ground. I am facing the
shaman and seated to the left of him. In his mind he
forms and projects a three-dimensional geometric
figure that I can perceive in my mind. I turn it around
in my mind observing it, then toss it back to the
shaman's mind. He smiles. I turn to my right and*

*notice my twin sitting there. The shaman tosses the
same mental image to the twin but the twin fumbles
the image, drops it. In his fear he has gone blank and
doesn't remember that he knows how to do all this. As
the twin drops the image he is immediately
transported ten feet under the solid ground. It seems as
if he has gone down a tiny crack in the ground where a
spring seeps up. I can sense his terror and suffocation
as I go over to look at the spot where he lies buried in
fear, amnesia and loss.*

The Place to Go Under

It's hard for me to see you here in this darkness. Pull a little closer to the fire where I can see your face. I have to tell you this. I have invested in loss, but I am not lost. I train and I take care of myself. On my way to black belt one of my teachers said, "Anything you choose to study and master can be a Way. But if it doesn't lead you to find out who you really are, then it's just clever behavior." Monkey like, jump up and down for an audience clever behavior. Clever, clever monkey business. Do you really Know, or are you just clever? There is no end to the desire of cleverness, a drug to the spirit.

We have clever athletes, clever businessmen, clever entertainers, clever artists, clever storytellers, clever spiritual teachers. If the words to this story don't point in a direction, don't point to the mountain, then I have failed. The words will only be clever manipulations of image and sound, signifying nothing.

> In the beginning those who knew the Tao
>   did not try to enlighten others,
> But kept it hidden.
> Why is it so hard to rule?
> Because people are so clever.

Rulers who try to use cleverness
Cheat the country.
Those who rule without cleverness
Are a blessing to the land.
These are the two alternatives.
Understanding these is Primal Virtue.
Primal Virtue is deep and far.
It leads all things back
Toward the great oneness.

—Lao Tsu

In ancient Chinese times the emperors were supposed to rule by the principle of *t'ien ming*, the "mandate of Heaven." The rulers were to serve as intermediaries between Heaven and the people, assume responsibility for the welfare of all their subjects. Proper rule was a way of virtue, a way to provide a setting and means for the people to work out their spiritual destiny.

By the 1830s China was disintegrating under the weight of the ravages of drug addiction. This great ravage was the product of the largest narcotics trafficking organization that the world has ever known, the British East India Company, forerunner and model of modern corporations. Tons of opium grown in India were freely peddled in China at great profit to the investors in the company. In India, the British Army brutally suppressed the rebellion against the rule of the company. In China the rulers tried to rise to the defense of their people but also fell to the cannons of the British Army in their role as defenders of the company. The army stayed to enforce the ravages of the drug trade and to enforce a new Treaty of Nanking that guaranteed not only the drugs, but the right to spread Christianity.

Soon after this Opium War, Clarence King's father, James, arrived in China. He was there to manage the family hong, or trading house, in Canton. He went back once to America for eighteen months to see Clarence as a little boy. A daughter was conceived, born and then she died. Another daughter was conceived. On James' return to China that daughter was born, then she also died. On a trip to the port of Amoy near the camphor island of Taiwan, the camphor used as a treatment for the addiction to opium, James caught a tropical fever and died.

Clarence was left alone with a teenage mother to raise him, left alone with a restless energy and intellect and an abiding fondness for things Asian. He was young, intelligent and suddenly saddled with an inheritance of loss, an entry into darkness without guidance. He had no choice but to search and explore, to look for something beyond definability. The family trading house had refused to traffic in opium, but soon changed its mind. After some years the hong was swept away in the tumult of conflict, the family left destitute and ruined.

A few miles past Lemon Cove is Lake Kaweah. The river used to flow freely through this area as it came down from the High Sierra and through the chaparral covered hills into the delta and the farmland. They dammed it in the 1960s with Terminus Dam built by the Army Corps of Engineers. Terminus was once the end of an electric railway that my grandmother's family would take on Sunday afternoons from the center of the valley to the sand beach of the Kaweah. The Mehrten family had another farmhouse in this area where the Kaweah spread among the willows, alders, cottonwoods and other dense growth as the river entered the valley floor. They called it the Swamp Ranch. There is a family story of one of Dutch Bill's daughters being stalked by a mountain lion through the marshy growth.

My father drove a giant earthmover here, helping to build this dam between bouts of his drinking. Strangely, to me, the brand name of the earthmover was Euclid—Euclid, the father of plane geometry and the Euclidean postulates. His postulates and axioms held sway and governed our perception of existence for over two thousand years till the advent of Riemann and Lobachevsky and Bolyai. They discovered that Euclid was true from a smaller and more limited perspective. As an observer's view was enlarged, expanded and questioned, other previously unseen relationships came into view. Now it seems that some of the fundamental elements are true only because we believe them to be true.

How like Euclid's Elements are our other systems of thought, our holy books and sacred ritual habits, our assumptions and postulates governing a small segment of reality? You have probably heard the story of the blind men and the elephant in which each man touches a different part of the beast and therefore has a different small description over which to quarrel. Imagine that you are a wise person, though still blind. You could stand back and hear all of the descriptions, then begin to visualize what sort of creature that this might be without having to be in opposition. You would be able to expand and really begin to see as the elephant took greater shape and form, the vision beginning to inhabit a portion of your mind.

The Euclid earthmover had tires that towered over my father's six-foot-two height and each tire cost more than our family car. I watched that dam go up bit by bit, and tried to visualize what this valley would look like drowned. This was the last uncontrolled source of water for Tulare Lake, there in the middle of what used to be Valle de los Tulares. Now the corporate farmers could fully reclaim the lakebed from its fullness without fear of flooding, without fear of loss. Somewhere below the water of the lake is the old village of Gaweah. Its secrets, its dark shadows now reinhabit a place beneath the surface. What shape, what form do crows assume beneath the water? On the water, thundering ski boats trace their paths through each other's wakes oblivious to the village of the dead beneath them, their weaving speed a narcotic.

Recently, the government has tried to retain more of the water for environmental reasons, but the corporate farmers of the lake bottom sued to retain their allotments, classifying the government action as a taking, without examining the depth of their own taking. They had forgotten that the lakebed wouldn't exist without the dam that had been built by the government with the people's money, the land bought at dirt cheap prices. They wanted the burden of loss to be felt everywhere else but in their economic bottom line.

Throughout the millennia, societies have generally been divided into four major groups. There were kings and other nobility, the priests and scholars, the warriors, and the craftsmen and farmers. Mostly, businessmen have stood as outsiders or even outcasts. Myths and stories accompany the main groups and describe how their social roles can be used as a spiritual path. There is a way of the king, a way of the warrior and a way of the farmer that if followed will lead to some kind of spiritual revelation or truth. There are no stories about the way of the corporate businessman. Perhaps it's because there is no motivating principle of being of service to the people and to the truth beneath the surface of things. It's all very, very clever monkey business.

Years ago, during the Reagan era, I lived in a small town in the Napa Valley and one evening I walked into my favorite little café/restaurant. The place was crowded and I was a single diner. I ended up sitting at a table with a young woman who worked in investments. During the conversation she began to tell me about the hierarchical ways of making money. The lowest form she said was to make money from what you did. The next higher level was to make money off of others and the highest form was to make money off of your money.

I didn't know what to say as I looked around the café. There used to be nothing open on this street at this evening hour till this café was built. I looked around the café again and remembered having to drive all of the way to Berkeley to get the wood to build the cabinets and the service bar. I remembered picking through the wood stock to find just the right pieces and trying to cover the oak and cherry well, because I was attempting to sneak it home between rainstorms. I also remembered building a redwood deck in the warm spring sun and how each sixteen-penny galvanized nail was struck just so, the nails driven home with a last tap that somehow sunk the head without marring the wood. In a time without thoughts one nail was struck and then another, with no time to admire or hold on to the perfection.

I remembered crawling under a house on a cold wet New Year's Eve replacing rotted joists. Suddenly there was only my breath in the midst of the cobwebs and the dirt. It didn't matter where I was or what I was doing. There was only my tidal breathing in and breathing out, tasting every molecule of the rush of air as my being expanded with joy. I continued working in the jewel-bedecked vastness of the moment beneath the floor as others walked aimlessly above.

I didn't know what to say to the woman sitting across from me. I knew that there was nothing in her experience as a broker to use as a touchstone. It was about the work of the hand as a discipline and path to knowing and it was all about the wonder of nothing, so there was nothing to say.

Hale Tharp was one of the first settlers in the Three Rivers area. Local Indians guided him deep into the mountains where he became the first white man to gaze on the Big Trees of Giant Forest. He was also the first white man to see Moro Rock and climb it. His daughter married Dutch Bill's brother's son. His homestead and ranch are now beneath the waters of the lake.

At the upper end of the lake is Slick Rock a massive sheet of exfoliating granite that slopes down the hillside into the river. My mother always said that there was an undertow here, but I don't know if it was true or not. Anyway, it was our excuse not to go swimming in this place. To the Yokuts this rock was called *Pahdin*, the Place to Go Under. The water hole was called *Ahdit Wishu*. Yokuts believed that an evil spirit lived beneath Pahdin and pulled swimmers beneath the water and drowned them. Did my mother know this story and did she have a personal name for this spirit that pulled one down?

After this whole valley itself was drowned I used to go fishing with my father in the lake. I always had to be careful of snagging my line on the submerged oaks and chaparral. What lurked with the fish in the shadows of those dead inundated oaks? All around us on the hillsides above the lakeshore was a great bathtub ring of debris that is endemic to these lakes behind dams on rivers that no longer run free.

The dam has now been raised by the Corps of Engineers so that at high water Pahdin is only partly to be seen above a lake surface that extends further back over the places that used to cascade and pool. The alien warm water bass push further up the river, eating, displacing the vigor of trout.

My life has certainly been full of dams and blockages. Like my parents and Dutch Bill I have staggered under the weight of debt and like Dutch Bill I have gone bankrupt. My concerns for money seemed to always drown out whatever small voice echoed from the depths. When I did go bankrupt I suffered so much shame and so felt the weight of generations that I ended up in the hospital with another hole in my gut. I didn't understand the workings of my internal Salmon Energy and its need to be in a flowing dynamic state. I felt that I had betrayed everyone in my life, and the worthlessness that I felt was like a concrete dam to the movement of my true life. I couldn't even pay to save my own life, my bill being paid by county welfare.

I ended up in a ward with several alcoholics and a senile old man who yelled out every hour in the night for a nurse to tell him where he was. "Nurse! Nurse! Where am I, where am I, where am I really, who am I really?" I knew that this was Hell and that I needed someone to help me understand the forces of which I was only partly aware. I offered a prayer. It seemed that some great hand was always pulling me down into the darkness, down below the surface of apparent things, down into the darkness below where others walk. Through it all, I have learned to see in the dimmest of lights.

As corporations have grown to take over the world they are perhaps exacting a price for those centuries of being outcast. They now have all the money and all of the power. There is a great "taking" in the world, but it's not what they suppose. It happens when we mindlessly remove parts of the landscape. It is as if we were to take a rough gouge, pierce our scalp and skull and scoop out a part of our mind, to strip-mine our own consciousness. We try to pull back our scalp into place in loose folds, try to smooth it over and hide what we have lost like a vain old man with a bad combover. This is the lobotomy of the Living Dead. Our mind is more than our brain, more than our desires.

I once met a man who worked for a while in a mental institution. He told me of a woman who had been lobotomized. Daily she would sit at a piano and begin to play the same song. Daily the song would end abruptly at the same exact point. The end of the song resided in that place that had been cut away. Can you remember the whole song?

If a scientist were to make a list of all the attributes of Christ, take the antithesis of those attributes and then compare them to known entities, global corporations would look a lot like the Antichrist. Like the British East India Company they would keep us in a stupor, keep us suspended in living death for the sake of commerce. Our demon expresses itself without mitigation in this pursuit of mindless wealth, visits our families and villages with destruction over and over.

Imagine knowing who you really are and being truly happy within your own mind. It is the only real revolutionary act. Imagine happiness without neediness, happiness without compulsive consumption to fill the gaping hole. There are those who wouldn't want you to find this complete mindedness, would work against it to preserve their authority or profit. Enough truly happy, complete minded people would be a threat to the world as we think we know it.

The corporations are clever beyond understanding, but still have no stories of the Way. They have no knowledge of the Mandate of Heaven, no desire to explore the world beneath the bottom line. They have no desire to go to Pahdin, the place below where others aimlessly walk.

The South Fork

Lean closer. I want to tell you this. We are at odds with the land because we are at odds with our minds. We are at odds with our minds because we are at odds with the land. The land supports the chaotic profusion of life that we fear. We dominate the land so that we can control life and therefore the complexity of our minds. We fear life because we fear our minds and don't want to choose how to go about living. We fear being responsible for our choices and so try to eliminate them. We want a list of rules, a list of formulations that will guarantee that we are doing the right thing, a list that will make sense of life.

Karma is just a measure of what we pay attention to and of what we ignore. We are afraid to know how totally responsible we are for our own destiny. We live in fear of that responsibility and go numb, mindlessly plow along from day to day, leaving a wreckage of life itself in our wake. We become the walking dead. Are you the living or the Living Dead that devours the bright and living? Is this something that you can answer truthfully?

Coyote is from the south, somewhere south of the border. No matter where he is standing he is from somewhere south of there. In this northern world, south always takes us deeper into swamps and jungles. Skin colors get darker. Maybe we remember that originally we all came from somewhere south of wherever we are now. South is the direction of the Unconscious, the direction of the teeming unbridled growth of all things, of all thoughts and impulses everywhere, of that which exists before thought.

North is up, south is down. South is the direction of Hell, the siren cacophony of all desires and impulses, of all sins and noble achievements singing at once. Somewhere the source exists lost and hidden in the storms. Hell is being a small boat without a rudder in this tossing sea. The only map says, "Here there be demons."

The sea can be calmed, the jungle penetrated. A rudder is necessary, a compass and knowledge of the stars. Some of my ancestors came around the Horn, others across the vast and seemingly endless plains. I am an inheritor of some kind of frontier knowledge. This sort of knowledge can be useful for one to go inward and south. Without this use of knowledge, life amounts to only clever survival, hard work with nothing truly gained except more hard work.

We are always fighting a Civil War between the North and the South, between the forces of enforced orthodoxy and financial order and the perceived disorder of the landscape of the mind.

In 1854 gold was discovered in the Kern River Canyon. Thousands of men roamed through the southern Sierra seeking their fortune. The merchants of Visalia began to supply the far flung camps of the mountain miners. The trails were so haphazard and inadequate that a new trail had to be built. The

Dennison Trail was created to snake through all the mining camps and eventually end in the Owens Valley, the first trans-Sierra route from the Great Valley.

In 1860 silver was discovered in the Cosos Mountains of the Owens Valley. A better, more direct trans-Sierra route was needed, so the Visalia merchants contracted to have the Jordan Trail built in 1861 and 1862 in order to send provisions to the other side of the mountain barrier. With the advent of the Civil War the silver ore from the Cosos was promised to the Confederacy. The Union Army reactivated Fort Independence in the Owens Valley to guard the Union's interest in the silver. The Union Army had to also staff a fort in Visalia because so many Pikes and other Southern transplants lived in the area and advocated for slavery and subjugation.

Supplying the remote Owens Valley outpost was a problem, so a new trail had to be constructed across the High Sierra in order that the merchants of Visalia could keep the Union Army equipped. In 1862 the Hockett Trail was begun. It began near Hale Tharp's ranch where Horse Creek met the Kaweah River not far from Pahdin (Slick Rock). The Hockett Trail followed the South Fork of the Kaweah to the Little Kern River, then circled around Sawtooth and the Great Western Divide and became the most direct route over the mountains.

Immediately after his failed attempt at climbing Mt. Whitney, Clarence King had to rush back to Visalia with an ailing William Brewer. King then decided to immediately attempt another summit assault on Whitney from the Kern side of the mountain. After enlisting two cavalrymen he set out for the mountains on July 14, 1864. His route took him directly along what would become the Mineral King Highway and directly by the place with no history where I grew up ninety years later. King passed on through the Mehrten lands as he approached the foothills. He would have ridden to Hale Tharp's ranch, though Tharp would probably have been summering at Giant Forest, and then turned at Horse Creek to follow the Hockett Trail across the Sierra.

King would have ascended from the river through the broken granite and red manzanita growth that gives way to oak, bay laurel, buckeye and redbud. In the spring these altitudes are covered with blooming poppies, lupine bushes as high as five feet or more and redbud trees in full riot. This was summer, though, the grass yellow and dry, seed pods hanging from the shrubs and trees except for the last straggling blooms of buckeye. As King finally entered the dark green coniferous forest he stopped at a creek to camp for the night. Nearby was another camp occupied by a group of hunters. When King visited their camp for a short time he was offered their whiskey and tall tales. He came away from the camp with the observation that, "I left them with a belief that my protoplasm and theirs must be different, in spite of Mr. Huxley."

Who knows, maybe these were my ancestors on a hunting trip in the mountains above their foothill ranch, Dutch Bill indulging his fondness for whiskey. What could they have had in common, the Yale educated, restless inveterate explorer and the obsessively hardworking German immigrant? There was this land beneath their feet. I wonder how tightlipped my great great grandfather might have been or whether the whiskey would have loosened his tongue enough so that stories might have sprung forth about strange spirits of the land, of spirits of rock and tree and seed. Maybe instead, he just became more numb to the cacophony of energies unsung.

A family of pig farmers fattening their swine in the mountains while the valley baked in the summer's hundred-degree heat inhabited another camp nearby. This migrant Pike family was like many people, mostly from the South, that inhabited the West at the time. They wandered from place to place, from one opportunity to the next perceived bigger opportunity, never quite sure where they were going. Nomadic tribes move across the landscape but they know every square mile of their range and they move with intent. These migrants just drifted toward the next imagined golden thing without knowing anything of where they were and little of where they had been. How many of us are like that, even though we live in comfortable houses? Never quite sure of where we are going and less sure of where we really are, life without intent. The Pike family was camped with a herd of three thousand squealing, rooting, shitting pigs beneath the forest canopy.

A judge from Visalia named Atwell had decided to raise prize hogs out on the island in Tulare Lake that came to bear his name. On the frontier, this succulent pork became a prize delicacy. The pigs rooted about the island and the marshes, shitting, urinating, befouling the old fisheries and food gathering places. After awhile the hogs developed a taste for freshwater clams and dove for them at every opportunity. Passersby could only see pig asses protruding from the water to the sky. Soon the pig meat had no market because of its rank fish taste. The hogs were let loose upon the land to go feral, immediately growing bristles and tusks, demonically stalking hunters from hiding places within the tules, the hunted become the hunter.

Are we all the same protoplasm? What makes us really

human, what makes a human mind? Is the course of evolution unequal or do we have a choice in the matter? If our evolution is now a matter of choice, then we are the only species that lives in multiple levels of evolution simultaneously. This is the beauty and horror of freedom. We are propelled by so many fears and half-truths. We are the Living Dead because we are less than half here and less than half alive. We have left so many little pieces of ourselves behind as we have drifted through the landscape of our lives. How much is left of you right here and right now? What means is there to go back and collect all the little broken pieces into our medicine bag so that we are just one piece, totally here, presenting one great face to this reality?

This story is my medicine bag. With all our pieces in place we can stop and choose to be aware of all this, be alive in all of this, to be fully human, no longer pushed and pulled about the landscape by forces that we try to ignore or don't really understand. Then we can begin to understand.

King left the camp of pork to continue on his quest for Whitney's peak. That night he camped at a bridge that crossed the main branch of the Kern River. From the Kern the group headed northward on an Indian path and then east toward their goal.

Even in summer the High Sierra can be treacherous to those not prepared. The high passes may be snowed in till August and a sudden snowstorm can strike and drop six inches of snow without warning in the middle of July. King chose a route too far to the east. He had been traveling head-long through the Sierra with a restless driven energy. He was only twenty-two and probably a bit full of himself. His goal was to conquer the peak, to be the first to the top of the highest point in the United States. After scrambling through ice, snow, scree, and boulders he found himself three to four hundred feet from the top of the helmet shaped dome that marks the peak of Whitney, blocked by a sheer granite wall. After surveying the great wall before him he decided to call it quits.

King wrote, "When I hung up the barometer a bitter wind was blowing; it hailed and snowed and the clouds closed in around me shutting off all view. I had been all day abroad and the fatigue and excitement exhausted me greatly, so much so that although chilled through I could scarcely prevent myself from lying down and sleeping. A strange carelessness came over me, making me reckless in the descent. I was obliged to make an effort to keep myself from running over the most dangerous debris slopes."

King had tried to conquer a mountain that he didn't know, didn't stop to measure its being. If he had really known the mountain he wouldn't have needed to conquer it. He could have just been there, just approached it, just walked around it. Maybe then the mountain would have invited him to the top. King turned back down the trail, back down the South Fork to the hot dusty plain of the Valley of the San Joaquin, back to the Kaweah River delta and the oak forest of Visalia.

Coyote beckons us southward and then confuses the way. Truth is the truth, the false is the false, with some truth in the heart of deception.

I am sitting in the dining room at Grandmother and Grandfather's house and I'm part of a circle of about

ten people. I look around and notice the faces of all the others around me. The faces are continually changing and the people's appearances are in a continual state of flux. I try to explain to them the nature of what it's like to live with one face, but everyone has a difficult time understanding. Bit by bit I begin to succeed.

Querencia

In the middle of Three Rivers, North Fork Drive turns off the main highway and crosses the main body of the Kaweah River. This is where the North Fork of the Kaweah meets the Middle Fork. The high hills on the northern side of the river were called *N'Hawntau*, Grizzly Bear Place, by the Pahdwishe to mark the scene where a grizzly killed one of their tribe. The Pahdwishe or Potwisha were a subtribe of the Paiute who lived on the other side of the Sierra. They had migrated over the high mountain passes along with other Paiute tribes and settled in the hills alongside the Yokuts in some sort of peaceful co-existence.

On occasion, I went with my father to the place where the forks of the river merged to fish for trout. I was fascinated by the way the water tumbled through the granite boulders, the way the rainbow trout flicked through the shadows in the river. There was something about the place that called to me, that made me want to be there.

The road parallels the North Fork on the western side for a few miles. It passes between small farms and ramshackle homes. To the west the land begins flat and then pitches steeply uphill. Some of the ground is open pasture, other places given over to the native growth of oak and pine. To the east along the river, houses are lost in thickets of wild grapevine and berry, crowded with all of the types of trees that like to hug the watercourse. Trees like river willow, sycamore and cottonwood. Along the way is an old cider mill that is no longer open. I drove up to the mill years ago, hours after my grandfather's funeral. There was a solace in the fresh squeezed juice from these hills.

The apple orchard seems dry, twisted and abandoned, and some of the acreage is now oranges. Some of the family once had orchards along here. The road soon crosses a small bridge over the North Fork and begins to rise above the riverine valley with all of its greenery. The greenery is itself a river that undulates at the base of these Sierran foothills. In summer the area surrounding the road is a stark contrast of yellow dryness studded with oak and exposed granite. Here the road narrows considerably and winds along the flanks of the hills past various horse and cattle ranches.

After a few miles there's a parking lot to the left with a large metal sign posted by the state that says "Advance Site." This marks the old location of the white tent city of Advance, an outpost of the Kaweah Colony. In 1886 a group of utopian Socialists from the Bay Area had founded the Kaweah Colony near Three Rivers in order to realize their dream of a worker's paradise. Tales of the vast timber tracts available in the Southern Sierra had lured them to this place. Their plan was to file claims on land in the Giant Forest region and use the timber proceeds to finance their utopia. Giant Forest was only accessible by old Indian foot trails and stock trails, so the colony would have to build a whole new road up the mountainside to the Sequoias. Advance was their road construction camp. They completed the road after four years of hard labor only to have their tracts made into Sequoia National Park very soon after.

From their point of view this was considered a taking. It's hard to imagine the amount of labor and pain that it took to build that road and how many hopes and dreams rose and fell over that period of time. The hills are rocky and rugged, hot and bone dry in the summer. They didn't have power equipment — just dynamite, picks, shovels, wheelbarrows, wagons and this dream of paradise somehow regained. But they had fallen victim to Karl Marx's greatest error: believing that humans are fundamentally economic animals. They didn't come here because they loved the place, but because there was timber to cut. They came for money and the money drove their dream. They didn't know that this was the Grizzly Bear Place, didn't know what the word Kaweah really meant, didn't really know that there had been villages here that had existed for over a thousand years in relative harmony and prosperity.

If we are really economic creatures why doesn't economics answer the fundamental questions? Who am I really and what am I doing here in this place? We are creatures who are always trying to find answers to these questions and in finding the answers build our soul. So how different were these Kaweah Colonists from the other side, that of capitalism and development? A few years ago I read a newspaper interview with the state senator from Fresno. He said, "Greed, I love greed. It's what makes the world go round." And I've heard this elsewhere. It's as if greed was all-knowing, could divine the needs of the people and meet them, but there is only one force that can do that. Even in the midst of prosperity we are left in pain. It's sad that the senator could camp by the river and not see it, him being so busy making plans to make money from it.

Did the Kaweah Colonists really see the North Fork that tumbled by their camp on its way from the high country? They worked too hard and fought too hard for their dream, unable to give themselves up to the knowing that all too quickly flowed by and was gone. By 1892 they were gone too, disillusioned, broke and broken, empty and saddled by loss. There are a few stone foundations left in Advance punctuated by piles of cow shit and wandering blank faced cows. I have walked on down to the river as the cows have bolted one way and another in dumb surprise. Their hooves chew the riverbank; the small beaches are spotted with their offal.

The old campsite is set amidst stands of oak and chaparral. I've seen pictures of the old city of white tents posed with proud dreaming families. It's come to this, a few stones and mounds of organic waste. There is an aura of sadness and incompleteness, of opportunity missed. Without attention the river goes by all too quickly.

A few miles further up the road another sign announces the Cherry Falls Recreation Area. A steep, deeply rutted dirt road turns off at this point and heads downhill toward the river, a road that almost demands a four-wheel drive vehicle with some clearance. A foot trail takes off from the parking lot. This trail also descends sharply through scattered oaks and through granite outcroppings, then passes between two large rock formations near the river. At the bottom of the trail the river forms a large pool at the base of a waterfall some fifteen to twenty feet high. The area is wooded and peaceful, but it hasn't always been so peaceful in the recent past.

Newly arrived ethnic gangs now patrol growing Great Valley towns. Some used to come here to the river to party and transact their trade. They jumped in the river, sold drugs by the river, but yet didn't see it. My great-great grandfather came here as an immigrant to escape the wars and conscriptions of the fractious kingdoms of Germany. He didn't come out of a love for this landscape, but rather what he could take from it or make from it. He had to bend it to his will, define it according to his beliefs about reality, much as the farmers of the lake bottom. So many drunks and sons of drunks take their wrath and their deep sorrow out on the land. Neither Dutch Bill nor the drug gangs could ever see the land for what it was and is. Most newcomers come from depleted lands and treat this new land in the same fashion as they treated the old. They have lost their sense of awe.

The poet Gary Snyder observed that we have to rediscover this land and the ways that we might become natives of this place and cease after all these centuries thinking and acting as newcomers and invaders. This land has no belief system, nothing holy or unholy. It simply exists as a sign of the deeper way.

We move so much from place to place, constant tourists and immigrants for greener pastures. We never stop long enough and silently enough to let our minds align with "place" and become natives and inhabitants. At that point we can begin to understand, to integrate the deeper workings of things.

There is a word in Spanish for part of all this. Querencia. It has no precise definition. I have seen it defined this way. "Querencia is the deep sense of inner well-being that comes from knowing a particular place on the Earth; its daily and seasonal patterns, its fruits and scents, its soils and birdsongs."

Querencia. A salmon smelling its home waters. If I know this place, I know God.

> The great Tao flows everywhere, both to the left
>   and to the right.
> The ten thousand things depend upon it; it holds
>   nothing back.
> It fulfills its purpose silently and makes no claim.
> It nourishes the ten thousand things,
> And is yet not their lord.
> It has no aim; it is very small.
> The ten thousand things return to it,
> Yet it is not their lord.
> It is very great.
> It does not show greatness,
> And is therefore truly great.
>
> —Lao Tsu

Mineral King

How is it that a person can truly begin to see, to drop the accumulated years of dead fabrication, drop the years of vacant emptiness? The Buddha once delivered a sermon by holding a single flower aloft. Kashyapa saw the flower and smiled. He understood as the others only puzzled and because of this became the first Zen Patriarch. The great understanding was passed directly from one mind to another.

You sit there across the fire. If I held a flower, what would you see? If I held a trace of gold before me, what would you see? If I held the inconspicuous seed of a Sequoia in the palm of my hand, would you finally see?

We want to see and are afraid to see. But seeing is only the beginning of why we're here. We then have to live the seeing. It is a tricky matter to sit and watch across the fire, to watch the face of what you fear the most, neither running away, nor being hypnotized and led to destruction.

Can we sit here long enough and just watch, to clearly see the destruction that you and I have wrought both inside and outside ourselves, then move on? There is just seeing, not fascination with seeing. There is only understanding, not paralyzing guilt with the horror that we've wrought. Can you do this?

Grandfather Went Riding

Grandfather was a cowboy near the turn
of this century
and rode the low Sierra of the central
San Joaquin
through manzanita and oak,
granite and yellowed grasses.
One day out riding he spied
a prairie dog upright and immobile
before some rattler hungry
and ready to strike.
He fired once, the snake quickly dismissed
with a look and some lead.
Then he paused and thought
and fired again
because the prairie dog was
"being such a fool."

As you pass on through Three Rivers you begin to rise high enough to see above the dense banks of tule fog that cloak the valley in winter. The fog is so dense at times that you can see no more than ten feet in front of your windshield, and headlights reflect back in a blinding glare. Sometimes on a clear winter night the valley will freeze, then the fog comes back dripping over subfreezing surfaces leaving a world of crystal shapes covering plants and posts in an otherwise gray world. I have never been so cold as on those days. I used to go out and prune vineyards midwinter with my grandfather in that tule cold and be pierced to the bone and beyond.

This is the condition of our minds. What stories have been told to us that can create such a winter and create such a fog?

What stories do we tell ourselves? Even in the passion heat of summer we exist as winter gray shapes in a dense and visionless place. What can pierce this fog?

Even rising to higher ground is no guarantee of seeing. Outside Three Rivers a right-hand turn takes you up the Mineral King Road that follows the course of the East Fork of the Kaweah. It is a tortuously steep twenty-six miles of narrow road and serpentine undulations that finally lead to Silver City and on into the valley of Mineral King beneath Sawtooth Peak and to the headwaters of the East Fork. Sawtooth anchors the southern end of the arc of the Great Western Divide.

At night along the steep remote road, trucks stop and let off their human cargo. Shadowy figures follow game trails to hidden terraced fields of marijuana hidden in the canopy of growth. The string of methamphetamine labs that have sprung up throughout the Great Valley finance the fields. The fields yield higher return and less exposure. The meth labs leave behind a toxic trail of chemical waste that requires massive cleanup, the chemicals leaching into water supplies. The marijuana fields near harvest are guarded with automatic weapons.

In the end nothing can ever really be controlled and repressed; manifestations spring forth in many places and many guises. It's probably better to have a few backyard farmers of weed than underground corporations of greed planting in the national parks, carrying weapons and surprising explorers of the Sierra unknown. Everyone has to choose how they approach or avoid the seeing. Prohibition avoids the deeper things, the deeper reason; the answer is in the teaching.

*I look from high above, across a landscape festooned
with totem like poles adorned at the top with raven's
heads that are painted in varying patterns of black
and white and point to the sky, stark against the colors
of the landscape. I am in a vehicle high on a narrow
road on the mountainside. We are on the left side of
the mountain and take a quick turn to the right. The
road abruptly ends and the vehicle disappears from the
dream. Dad suddenly appears next to me. There is a
great drop-off beneath us and directly above us three
dislodged boulders are coming down in an avalanche
of granite. All of the boulders are in midair. I
unhesitatingly jump outward in a soaring leap, and
then push off the largest rock in midair with my feet so
that it lands further outward and away from us. The
other two land harmlessly. I see that my father has
landed unhurt. I land further out in a grassy patch on
top of a rock formation and as I land we then jump
together over a ravine. Father congratulates me on
pushing the rock away. I tell him I knew that if I
pushed off hard I would land in a better place to set up
the next jump, billiard-like. My father shows no signs
of drunkenness or self-pity; he seems to have his own
mastery of the Energy. It is the first time that I
remember seeing him like this in a dream.*

In 1862 Harry Parole became a game hunter for the crew
building the Hockett Trail that wound up the South Fork.

While out hunting from a campsite on the Little Kern River he spied a gap flanked by two peaks of equal height. He and his Paiute helper went to explore. When they crossed the windy gap they dropped down into the Eden of Mineral King. The animals were so unaccustomed to the sight of men that they didn't flee. Of greatest importance was the fact that everywhere the valley showed the signs of gold.

The Wuchumne once had a village, Coachnaumeu, down on the Kaweah across the river from Gawea, the village of the Crow Cry People. It too was submerged beneath the rising waters of the flood. A branch of the tribe lived up on the East Fork and during summers moved camp to the area of Silver City. They hunted the high reaches of Mineral King. During that time the people took greater and greater refuge in the high country as the land suffered devastating droughts of 140 and 200 years in length.

But, something happened. Who can know now? Maybe a sudden early and harsh drought-breaking winter storm caught the tribe at high altitude where many perished, or maybe a vision just told them it was time to go. The place became cursed, carried a taboo of unknown origin, unknown even to the tribes of the nineteenth century. The Indians of the Mineral King were gone long before Harry Parole got there. The animals had forgotten the forays of the hunting parties, and the land showed little trace of the passing, save a few old faint campsites and middens, some scattered scraps of black arrowhead obsidian from the eastern side of the mountains.

When my grandmother died, a very young minister who had really never known her performed her funeral. The minister's wife asked about my grandmother's life, shocked to learn that my grandmother used to accompany my grandfather on his annual horse-packed deer hunting trips to the high Mineral King. Grandfather used to help drive cattle to the area as a young man in the early years of the 1900s. He was known as "One Shot" Harry because of his training as a World War I sniper. He used a single shot bolt action 30-06 and was always successful.

If you stand in the Mineral King Valley, there is a sense of the magic of high mountain places. It is surrounded on three sides by the high granite, bare above timberline peaks. Empire Mountain, Sawtooth Peak, Mineral Peak, Rainbow Mountain, Florence Peak, Vandever Mountain, White Chief Peak. The surrounding peaks together are called the Sawtooth Circle. In the high granite basins of the peaks are crystal clear lakes that empty down into the valley and form the East Fork of the Kaweah. Franklin Lakes and Eagle Lake and White Chief Lake and Crystal Lake and Mosquito Lakes, lakes that were originally so high and remote that fish life had been unable to yet reach them. In 1874 an early prospector named Uncle Wiley Watson came up from the little Kern with four trout in his coffeepot, then sent them flashing down their way into the East Fork populating the whole valley and eventually the high lake basins of the circling peaks.

At the western end of the valley the land falls away in an escarpment, the river plunging over the edge and downward in scenic granite-laced falls. The river continues its steep descent for miles in falling steps that gradually ease, but the water still flows madly through rapids and pools in the rock till it meets the Middle Fork. The river starts in the pure granite high country, flows down through the evergreen forest of

Sequoia, fir and pine near Silver City, and then through oak, buckeye and bright spring flame of redbud. In the early summer the river sparkles like a river of silver against the exposed granite. The gold of summer dry grasses is punctuated by the last blooming buckeyes. Maybe a last straggling wildflower of red or purple protrudes through the yellow grass.

At the eastern end of the valley, Farewell Gap looms at the bottom of the V formed by the two peaks that so attracted Harry Parole in the first place. To the north, Sawtooth Pass and Timber Gap serve as entries to the Great Western Divide.

Silver City lies in the conifer forest that opens to the meadows of the valley where quaking aspen, alder and willow line the banks of the creeks and river. During the winter, snow can accumulate as deep as fifty feet. The steep, relatively bare slopes of Mineral King yield periodic avalanches that pour down one side of the valley walls, swoop across the narrow meadow floor and trigger an answering cascade of snow and ice from the other side. The tumbling snow melts in the heat of the fall, and then refreezes in a quick set of icy concrete around whatever is in its path.

For a while Harry Parole kept his secret to himself, but gradually the word leaked out. Some people came in over Farewell Gap while others tried the arduous route up the East Fork. If you follow the East Fork you have to face the verticality of the falls. If you move away from the river and up to the ridges, the chaparral growth of manzanita and buckbrush, sagebrush and chinquapin is so dense that it seems only a rabbit could penetrate it. But somehow people have always found a way when gold is in the air.

In August 1872, three would-be prospectors were camped

on the Little Kern. While sitting around the campfire a vision came before them. Rising up was the spirit of a great white Indian. He pointed to the north in the direction of the gap between the peaks of equal height that Harry Parole had crossed ten years before. He told them of a place where the mountains were red and white and black, where there were shafts and caverns streaked with the glint of gold. At the spirit's behest the men took horses and ropes to follow the vision through the night.

They followed an impossibly difficult and dark nighttime path up through the canyon and over the pass till they found themselves at the top of a steep granite wall. From there they roped their way down to the base and found themselves at a great circular canyon. There in the middle the vision gestured around with outstretched arms, the sun rose and the White Chief spirit vanished with the arrival of the light. The men hurriedly turned back to civilization to stake their claim. They named it the White Chief Mine.

The merchants of Visalia, in their usual haste where profits were concerned, rushed to build a road into the new land of mineral plenty. First the serpentine stock trail was made into a tortuously convoluted wagon road, which was then straightened by Chinese labor. The mile-and-a-half-long River Grade eliminated many switchbacks, but ascended at a 42 percent slope over solid stone blasted from the face of the mountain. Iron shod horses and iron clad wagon wheels would slide on the granite with the wagons threatening to slip back down the hill if the horses stopped on the grade. To lighten the load, passengers had to get out and walk. They walked ahead of the rig lest it break loose and tumble back downhill on them in an ass over teakettle jumble of wagon and horses. It took three hours for a team and wagon to climb that mile and a half.

"Coyote hole" diggings dotted the steep slopes of the Mineral King Valley, which the miners called Beulah, the biblical Promised Land. Maybe the coyote holes were called such because they resembled the wild canine dens or maybe because of their seductively sweet false promise in the land of great promise. The ore tailings could fall away down the slopes, sometimes showering rocks on miners and cabins below. A law was passed that miners had to keep their rocks on their own land.

Life was hard and money was scarce. The cost of extraction was prohibitive even though there was gold in Beulah. In a high altitude world of hard work and bad whiskey, hangovers were also hard and very real. The boys of camp hunted the marshy bog for the northern rubber boa, a lumpy dark coffee colored snake that seemed to have two heads, a small twenty-inch relative of the great anaconda. Miners prized the smallest snakes, especially the ones with a well-marked head on the tail. The miners carried the boas next to their bodies as a curative for the DTs and shakes, the snakes of this Eden used to moderate the curse of the miner's dreams. As a boy I remember having to nurse my father through those times of the shakes and self pity, and console him through his sense of failure, his fear of the dark forest at night and the incessant beatings of the Energy. The relief of whiskey and, in turn, the relief from its bad effects, turned more profit than all the mines.

Visalia's Judge Atwell, he of Atwell Island and airborne pig-ass fame, built a new sawmill near Silver City. The surrounding Sequoia groves began to be cut and milled.

Corporations rose and fell fueled by dreams of wealth that could never be smelted down and poured into reality at this altitude. Had the great White Chief lied? What indeed was his message? Where was the gold, the great abundance where the mountains were red and white and black? A short distance over Sawtooth Pass lays the Great Western Divide backed by the Kaweah Peaks. Red Kaweah, Black Kaweah, Kaweah Queen. Can I be more fortunate than the old miners in the peaks of Mineral King? Ravens claim the higher altitudes from cousin crow, their cry softer, throatier, almost apologetic in comparison. They circle on the mountain thermals and still beckon.

Could it be that Coyote had donned the form of White Chief (after all he was white) and left the seekers a little short of the mark, testing their ability to see, testing their ability to be tempted? Choices, choices, suddenly there were choices. The vision had not pointed to the ground where it stood but had gestured around in every direction to the surrounding peaks. Which form of gold would they choose, which door would they choose?

I have heard that all of the gold ever discovered can fit into a cube forty feet on each edge. The real gold can expand far beyond that, the mind its only limitation.

We have to get back to Parsifal again. Parsifal had been given the quest of finding the Holy Grail and so had traveled far in his journeys. After all this time and great distance he found a man fishing in a boat on a lake, alone in the gray mist and fog. Parsifal had finally stumbled upon the Fisher King. The old man invited him to stay the night at his abode, which is "down the road a little way, turn left across the drawbridge."

The moment that Parsifal entered the castle the whole court turned out to greet him. Soon the great nightly ceremony commenced once again as it always has and always will until all have found the Grail. A maiden carried the lance that had pierced the side of Christ, and another maiden carried the paten, which had born the bread of the Last Supper.

Finally the last maiden appeared and carried the Holy Grail, the vessel that had contained the wine of the Last Supper. It was the fount of life itself, the great cornucopia. All who were present were given what they wished from the Grail Cup even before they could give voice. All save the Fisher King, who could not drink from the Grail because of his wound. As the others were filled, his suffering intensified to yet another level. He was like a child on an icy day with his nose pressed to the window, separated from the warmth and blessings on the other side. Have you ever felt so separated from the essence of life itself?

What was the key to this blessing? Parsifal's teacher Gournamond had instructed him that if he found the Grail that he was to ask one question.

"Whom does the Grail serve?"

Would all of the blessings of life serve the one true face, the large self, the true self? Or would the blessings be claimed by one of the pain-ridden small egos that spring up in myriad manifestations like weeds around our stories of loss?

Parsifal froze, afraid to be so bold. In his fear of judgment and failure he had gone blank and didn't remember that he knew all of this. Like choosing the wrong door or seeping down a crack in the ground in fear, amnesia and loss, he was cast out alone on the road to wander after the Grail again, left to wonder if he would ever come upon it once more and taste the true essence of life. When he awoke the castle was gone and the Grail was gone. The road stretched endlessly ahead.

Do you know whom or what your life energy serves?

In the years right before Mineral King was joined to Sequoia National Park, the Walt Disney Corporation almost made the valley into a ski resort with entertainment and distraction, cleverness and recreation brought to the high country. For myself, I prefer backcountry skiing with every turn earned by energy expended.

I once worked as a carpenter in the Napa Valley vineyard home of Mrs. Disney many years after her husband's death. As I silently worked on the locks on her bedroom doors I noticed with a start the picture of Walt staring at me from the dresser, conjuring up years of memories of myself mesmerized, entranced in front of the television. Uncle Walt. As I looked out the window a great blue heron stood stoically on a dock in the reservoir a hundred feet away, fishing. The dock swayed in the breeze, the heron just stood fishing. It knew nothing of the master of fantasy and illusion nor did it have Technicolor dreams of mice in red shorts. It carried no wound. It was just a heron. It just fished. The breeze blew by, the water rippled. The heron fished.

Are you this real?

Chappo

It can be frightening to sit in the dark and the firelight. Though it may seem strange, there are times that it's easier to see in the darkness than in the light. How is it that in the light of day we can be so blind to a landscape that contains all that we seek?

For one hundred million years after what think of as the beginning of time the universe was a black featureless void of dark matter with wisps of hydrogen and helium curling through. The dark matter came together and began to clump, attracted the hydrogen into denser and denser clouds that ignited, and formed giant stars. In the furnace of these stars were forged the heavier elements. These great stars lived for only a short while, then exploded into supernovas, seeding the universe with the necessary heavy elements to create stars as we know them, this planet and life, this moment where we are together. Light as we know it came through the dark night, it was a gift of the coming together of the dark mysterious matter. Light grows out from the darkness like a plant from the dark humus of the earth. Light does not triumph.

I have heard a medieval saying that states, "Light that emerges out of the darkness is the Christ. Light that ignores the dark or triumphs over the dark is the Antichrist." Triumph does not unite, but rather further fractures the world.

Does anything dark and mysterious begin to draw together in the night of your mind? Few people make it to this fire and through the night, yet, for the sake of our survival, many must. Why so few?

Confucius said of Lao Tsu: "I know a bird can fly, a fish can swim, an animal can run. For that which runs a net can be made; for that which swims a line can be made; for that which flies a corded arrow can be made. But the dragon's ascent into heaven on the wind and the clouds is something that is beyond my knowledge. Today I have seen Lao Tsu who is perhaps like a dragon."

Lao Tsu is shrouded in mystery. He existed at about the time of the Buddha. Legend tells us that he was the keeper of the royal archives. When he found that not many paid heed to his knowledge or could learn from his teachings, and sensing the decay of the society of which he was a part, he chose to leave. As he rode away into the great western desert, Yin Hsi, the gatekeeper at the frontier, stopped Lao Tsu. Yin Hsi knew who Lao Tsu was and of his great reputation for wisdom. Yin Hsi begged him to write down the essential teachings before he departed. Thus was born the Tao Te Ching.

Empty yourself of everything.
Let the mind become still.
The ten thousand things rise and fall while the Self
   watches their return.
They grow and flourish and then return to the source.
Returning to the source is stillness, which is the way of
   nature.
The way of nature is unchanging.

Knowing constancy is insight.
Not knowing constancy leads to disaster.
Knowing constancy, the mind is open.
With an open mind, you will be openhearted.
Being openhearted, you will act royally.
Being royal, you will attain the divine.
Being divine, you will be at one with the Tao.
Being at one with the Tao is eternal.
And though the body dies, the Tao will never pass away.

—Lao Tsu

Why do so few make it through this night and into the light? The great power of our minds is mostly harnessed to making excuses, excuses for the sad state of our existence. One of the greatest excuses is, "This is just who I am." Who is it that sits before me? The True One or the excuse? Empty yourself of everything.

As you drive toward Sequoia along the highway it follows the course of the Middle Fork of the Kaweah. After passing the park entrance you soon arrive at Hospital Rock. The river courses through and over giant boulders here, forming great pools and drops. During spring runoff a misstep could find you swept fatally downstream. Away from the river are more great rocks with near-obscured ancient paintings that the Indians called Hawyu. Under Hospital Rock itself is a natural cavern.

I came here as a Boy Scout in the late fifties. We camped in a giant umbrella tent during a days-long deluge. I was told that Indians once camped here, but that was all that anyone knew. Our scoutmasters knew little or nothing about the outdoors or how to prepare us for it, knew nothing of how to really see this place. There were so many things that I wanted to know, but there was so little offered. We would walk out on the granite boulders between rainstorms, mindful not to slip on the lichen and leaves. One evening I found a tick burrowed into my upper arm. The scoutmaster approached with a solution. He brought his glowing cigarette closer with the idea that the heat would cause the tick to back out. The glowing end came too close, incinerating the tick and burning my arm. My arm still carries the scar of that ignorance of how to be in this reality.

In 1911, a year before he died, Hale Tharp recounted his early days in the Sierra foothills and in the high mountains themselves. When he arrived in 1856 there were over two thousand Indians living along the Kaweah above Lemon Cove, and Hospital Rock was the seat of government for the Potwisha or Paudwisha tribe of the Western Mono. He stated that the camp was never vacated during any of the seasons and that campfires were kept continually burning. The old, the sick and young mothers with children remained there in camp year-round.

Though Tharp was described as a crusty pioneer with a quick temper who often wore two six shooters, he became close friends with Chappo, the chief of the Potwisha. Tharp paid his first visit to Hospital Rock in 1858. It took about eight hours to ride there along the narrow footpaths from his Three Rivers ranch beneath the lake.

In Tharp's words, "When I arrived at the camp, Chief Chappo and his men extended me a cordial welcome and gave me the best that the camp afforded. He called out every individual in the camp and introduced me to them all. There were over six hundred Indians then living at the camp. My arrival excited most of the Indians as I was the only white person that had ever visited their camp, and only a few leaders had ever seen a white person before. As for myself, I did not attract half as much attention as did my horse and saddle, my weapons, and the clothing I wore. These were all new to most of the Indians as they had never seen such things before.

"On the following morning Chappo showed me all through his camp and explained its many advantages over others. It was the cleanest camp I have ever seen. He showed me the house-rock, the spring, the river, the sweat house, and what extra stores of food, clothing and other supplies he had. The supplies were all stored nicely under the rock, leaving just enough space for two beds. In one of the beds was a woman with a broken leg and in another was a woman with a very young baby. The bed mattresses were bear robes, and the quilt coverings were of nice white buckskins. Nearly all of the Indians wore buckskin suits. They had great quantities of acorns, meats, medical herbs and other supplies stored under the rock. There was no smoke on the room ceilings then. This was caused by whites camping there after the Indians left. He showed me the paintings on the rock, and asked me to tell him what they meant. He said that none of his people understand them or know of what material they were made. He had given orders that none of the Indians should touch them, as undoubtedly they had been put there by some people before their time, and that maybe some day some person would come along and tell them what they meant.

"By the spring of 1862, quite a number of the whites had settled in the Three Rivers area. Then, too, the Indians had contracted contagious diseases from the whites, such as measles, scarlet fever and smallpox, and they died off by the hundreds. I helped to bury twenty-seven in one day up on the old Sam Kelly place. About this time Chief Chappo and some of his men came to see me and asked me to try to stop the whites from coming into their country. When I said that it was impossible, they all sat down and cried. They told me that their people loved this country, did not want to leave it, and knew not where to go.

"A few days later Chappo came to me with tears in his eyes and told me that they had decided not to fight the whites but would leave the country. From that time on they moved out little by little and from time to time till they were all gone. I think that by the summer of 1863 the Indians had left the district. Their Hospital Rock camp was the last vacated and they left it clean as a ribbon. I don't know what has become of them now."

The image of Chappo and his men falling to the ground in tears moves me to great tears. Have you ever loved a place as much as this, have you ever known its intimacy? Have you ever loved the landscape of your own mind as much as this, to not allow it to be bought or sold, its fluid movement dammed or polluted? Have you ever known this greatest intimacy? Taking the land from the Potwisha was like a savage lobotomy of their mind and soul.

But where is home, where is the land of origin before the land of birth? What have we lost, what have we lost? I see the hollow eyes in the faces of the Walking Dead. They eat your dreams, they eat your knowing, they eat your eyes and soul.

Chappo and his people left from the lands of the Middle Kaweah as Lao Tsu had left for the western desert. They left silently because no one would hear them or see them. Lao Tsu left the traces of his teaching, but the Potwisha left only a clean and silent camp adorned with a painting so old that even they didn't know its meaning. Their spirits move about, the silence beckons. The silence can have a voice and your real voice is the sound.

It is dangerous to love your home so much, to love the water cascading through boulders in sunlight, oak trees hanging with lichen, redbuds bursting in spring, golden poppies, purple lupine, stark buckeyes hanging from bare branches in autumn. The hollow-eyed will curse you as being a nature lover, a pagan who blocks comfort and progress, a person who hates mankind. But I know this. I am not a nature lover. I am nature. Because I am nature I understand what it is to be truly human. I thank God for that. God? God, you say? Can I tell you about God?

No. No one can really tell you about God. You have to go there for yourself. Everyone has to go there for themselves. There are no shortcuts, no indulgences, no martyrdom, no blessing, no mantra, no sutra, no liturgy, no guarantee. There is no hymn to sing to save you. There is only loving and being loved, there is also the fire and the demon and the courage of your soul. It is not a sin to be human. The greatest sin is to avoid understanding what it means to be human.

This is the nature of being human, evolution through courage and choice, not just the mathematical vagaries of probability and chance coursing through the DNA. We can choose not to be hollow-eyed, we can choose to be really human, we can choose to be full and abundant-minded.

I see a chimpanzee in the center of a small clearing in the jungle. It has taken a shit there in the middle of its clear space. I say, "Watch him become aware of himself." As I walk up to the chimp he becomes aware of the shit and then aware of me. It tries to pick up the waste to move it, but gets some on its hands. I kneel down to show the chimp how to shake it off and then rub his hands in the sand.

I then walk over to a faucet and turn it on. Over and over I show the chimp how to wash its hands. The chimp suddenly understands and proceeds to wash its hands. Without prompting, the chimp then begins to wash off the rest of its body. At this point the chimp no longer has any hair and looks like a small human. It begins to talk and communicate with simple words, yet conveys complex thoughts.

What waste, what excrement are we willing to live in before we chose to move on down the human road?

Soon after Clarence King left Thomas' Sawmill Ranch in 1864 on his horse Kaweah he came across an Indian funeral near the Sequoia groves. Buck the chief had just lost his wife Old Sally and she was to be cremated there by the great cinnamon-barked trees. The next morning after the pyre, King went looking for Buck, the fire still smoldering, the coals still hot. He came upon Buck, dirty, bloated, and drunk, lying with some new young wife. Aghast, King quickly concluded that, "the Quakers would have to work a great reformation in the

Indian before he is really fit to be exterminated."

It could have been that these were a few of the remaining Potwisha who had wandered away from Hospital Rock in their self-enforced diaspora. King thought he was seeing the true nature of the Indian spirit. What he saw were people that had already been infected by the flesh and soul-eating bacteria of the conquering hollow ones, people reduced to living in a filthy camp in their own waste. This is the not-seeing, this is the soul consumed.

The highway curves to the left at the parking lot for Hospital Rock. Tourists wonder at the meaning of the paintings, glimpse the grinding holes, walk down to the river, and then hurry on. In that brief moment did they love this place, understand its fullness? Chappo is still here amidst the oak and granite looking to tell his story. His tears fall and softly rustle in the dry leaves. The river cascades, pools, then rushes by.

Overhead looms the mass of Moro Rock, a short distance vertically as a crow or raven flies, but the highway to it a long, winding and switchbacked road.

Wahah Yahkow

Yes, it's hard to make it through this night, to face all that you fear the most, to face all of the chaos and uncertainty, to face the impulse to make everything the way you want it to be. The fear can be multiplied, the difficulty compounded. Imagine your fear spreading outward till it meets the fears of all others in all places. The multiplicity of fears fold and curl into something else, something darker, more forbidding, something that lurks below the edge of consciousness in everyone and gains a life of its own. We give it a name, a demonic name. We live in deathly fear of it.

The dark and forbidding whispers to us, whether we consciously hear or not. Some of us cannot shut it out. Some hear all the voices of all the fear in the world as if every radio station came in at once. If we make it through our own night we can remove our portion, our voice, from the dark and forbidding collective cacophony of fear.

If you have not made it through the demon night and faced the darkest of things, then as you walk down the street and notice some disheveled haunted person at the margin of life, stop and bow silently in their direction. In your mind ask for forgiveness. The darkness that you have ignored, your fear compounded with all other fear, echoes and vibrates through them. They suffer in part for you, for your unresolved sins.

I cannot be fully enlightened till everyone is. We share a common mind. As free as I might be from my own fear, I am still privy to your fear, to everyone's fear. I work to keep my mind clear. It would be far easier if we did it together. We must collectively set things straight.

There is no such thing as private fear and private hell; there exists no luxury of isolation. It all echoes through a larger mind that we cannot see. So much fear, so many obstacles and so few make it through the night. Yet we all must make it. Do you have the courage to which few can lay claim? Better to remain asleep than to lose courage and try to quit. The pain of the half-aware person without courage is great, almost better to die.

We have come back to where this story started. *Wahah Yahkow*, "High Rock." This is the native name for Moro Rock. In 1858 when Hale Tharp visited Chappo at Hospital Rock, the Potwisha brought him to this area where he became the first white man to see the great Sequoias of Giant Forest and to see Moro Rock. At Log Meadow, a short distance from Crescent Meadow, Tharp found a fallen giant hollow Sequoia in the midst of lush grass with a small stream nearby. The hollow part of the great log was about 56 feet long and was 8 feet high at the highest point and tapered to 4 feet at the back. It was all part of a tree that originally was 24 feet in diameter at the base and stood 311 feet tall. Tharp outfitted the log with a door, window, stone fireplace and furniture. He summered there in the meadow every summer with his animals till the park was formed in 1890.

In 1875 John Muir visited Sequoia and described meeting a horseman at Log Meadow and being invited to the man's home. "I returned to my own camp, saddled Brownie, and by the middle of the afternoon discovered his noble den in a fallen sequoia hollowed by fire—a spacious log house of one log, carbon lined, centuries old, yet sweet and fresh, weather proof, likely to outlast the most durable castle, and commanding a view of garden and grove grander far than the richest king ever enjoyed."

In 1861 Tharp and his two stepsons became the first white men to climb Moro Rock. In 1872 or 1873 Tharp's daughter Fanny became the first white woman to climb the rock. She did this while she was still a teenager and before she married into the Mehrten family. Wooden steps were constructed to the top in 1917 and later replaced by a cable. During the Great Depression steps were created in and on the rock by the C.C.C. and the W.P.A. When I stand at the top of the rock I can look toward the thirty-two peaks of the Great Western Divide and then across the canyon of the Middle Fork to the granite turrets and spires of Castle Rocks. The Indians called Castle Rocks, *Lungnotim*, "The Undertakers." When I see Castle Rocks I think of the Grail Castle and I think of an old man whom I once met.

Not long after I had collapsed under the weight of my bankruptcy and the pain of the incessant beating of Energy in my too small life, I was talking to an older friend of mine, a kindly mentor. I mentioned that Barbara and I were going to hear Robert Johnson, the Jungian psychologist, speak. Johnson is the author of *He*, a book about Parsifal and the legend of the Holy Grail. This friend said, "You have to talk to him, engage the man in conversation. You might find it interesting." Reluctantly I said that I would, but like a kid with his fingers crossed. I was too self-conscious and had no intention of doing it at all.

Barbara and I arrived for the weekend-long event—the room was already full with hundreds of people as we looked for a place to sit. Somehow in a small miracle there were two seats available in the second row a little to the left of the lectern. Johnson soon started his talk by recounting parts of the Grail legend and what it meant to cross the drawbridge and enter the Grail Castle. I eagerly followed the story of Parsifal in his search as I recognized my own deep kinship. Johnson then talked about the wound of the Fisher King and what it meant to our world, then asked the question, "Where did this wound come from?" At that moment I knew that I knew the answer.

Johnson then told a story of an Indian boy named One-Two Man who was raised by his grandmother. He paused in his telling. "And you know," he said, "this is significant, this boy being raised by his grandmother. To be raised, to be taught by the grandparents is to be raised by the Unconscious and cast immediately into the spirit world. The house of the grandparents is the Spirit House. The boy doesn't know the ways of the parents, the ways of the world." He smiled saying, "I was raised by my grandmother."

After he finished speaking, there was a break so I turned aside to talk with Barbara. I turned back to the front and old man Johnson was sitting right there in the chair in front of me, staring ahead. I remembered my promise, moved my lips, but could say nothing. I couldn't make a sound. At that moment he turned, and then said, "Did you say something?" Startled, I could only say, "No." He turned back to looking idly ahead.

Finally I worked up my courage and barely managed, "Dr. Johnson, I was told that I should speak to you and . . ." I mumbled on trying to sound rational. Much to my surprise he began to talk to me. After a few moments of talk he said, "Marie-Louise von Franz once taught me a trick about giving these lectures. She said that I should pick out the face of someone that I liked and speak directly to that person. I hope you don't mind that I chose you."

I was suddenly and profoundly stunned. This couldn't be happening. I was a failure and this great man who had studied with Jung was choosing me, at least for this moment. The next speaker came on and lectured for a while, but I couldn't focus on her words. I was elsewhere. After she finished I tapped the old man on the shoulder. "This whole thing overwhelms me, it shocks my mind." He replied, "I meant for it to. You are a great man." A pause. "Somebody once did that for me. One day you will have to do it for another." Again I was stunned. I could sense the flow of some energy coming to me. Who knows where it started and where it would all go, the moment flowed through my mind. I felt as if an earthquake of some immense proportion had leveled me.

I went home that night still trying to comprehend the whole affair. Whatever it was seemed so complete that I could ask for nothing more. The next morning it felt like the whole thing had been a dream that could not have happened. I wrote a note to him. "Thank you, Grandfather, I accept this responsibility."

Back at the lecture I sheepishly handed him the note. He

looked at me and inquired, "Where are you sitting. I need some energy this morning. May I borrow yours?"

The day wore on and I didn't see him again. Everyone assumed that he was gone because he was flying to India that afternoon. I could feel my sadness, but I couldn't ask for anything more. When the conference was over I stood alone in the lobby, looking around at the aftermath. Johnson suddenly swept in through the front door with his bags, brushed off several ladies who tried to stop him and made a line directly to me. He dropped his bags and embraced me. Then he picked up his bags and walked away. There were no words, just the gesture. I was close to tears. That memory is now with me like the fields and mountains of my youth.

As I awake in the dream, Robert Johnson comes into the room. It seems as if he has come from an elevator. The room is dark and I reach out and manage to touch him. As I do he puts his arm around me and we walk through a doorway into a more lighted room.

I once wrote to Dr. Johnson and told him of the view from Moro Rock looking out toward the Great Western Divide. He responded that the view from atop the granite monolith was one of his favorite vistas and that he went there whenever he could. Later I found that as a child he had lost one of his legs, yet he still managed to climb the 350 steps to return to the great vista. In the face of this effort what do we let get in the way of our seeing? After he told me of his fondness for the view I realized that when I was a child and had wished for someone to talk to about the deeper things, he had been driving unseen down the highway that goes past my old home and follows the course of the Kaweah and then goes on to Moro Rock.

I have no way of knowing how he struck me with such timing and clarity. Some things are just a mystery. All I know is that I suddenly felt seen and touched in a way that I had never felt seen and touched before. He saw my spirit and not my circumstances. After that time I slowly began to accept the experience of who I really am. I had searched through many spiritual teachers and traditions. Yet it took just an old man and an embrace of deep regard and love to help me find myself. There were no traditions, no ritual forms to this knowing. I have kept the promise to the old man in my heart, that I would do all this for another. It's what motivates me to sit through the long night at this fire.

My family has suffered for lack of deep touching, both physically and in the soul. If you were seen and touched at such depth how would you respond? If you were seen at such depth when you were young, who would you be now, how would your experience of life manifest itself? Would you have the same empty longing or would you finally know the fullness of who you are? Would you be able to reflect some greatness of spirit, true nobility? Could you then touch another and on and on? Would our world suffer less, would Tulare Lake with its myriad forms of life be restored in the abundant wetlands of our mind?

Imagine the return of the rivers of the Great Valley, the salmon making their way upstream, their silver current of

Christ energy coursing through the restored neural networks of our being. It's time that we awoke from our night of the pitchfork-wielding Living Dead.

Years ago I stood atop Moro Rock with my new family and looked out over the canyon of the Middle Fork of the Kaweah for the first time in my life. My father had always been too tired of life, his life a tunnel vision of pain, and my mother too tired of taking care of him and my sister to take me up the flight of steps so we could take in the panoramic vision of our lives and our legacy. Looking out over the sweeping expanse I decided that I had to penetrate the backcountry and find out for myself exactly what lay there at the headwaters of the Kaweah in the Great Western Divide.

As I stood atop this rock with my wife and daughter I began to tell them of my Sequoia legacy and of Dutch Bill. My daughter took it all in with awe as if this too were part of her, even though in fact she is not my biological daughter. She was ten at the time and I watched carefully as she reveled, enraptured by the great view, my hand poised to catch her if she should slip at such a great height.

I don't know where I would be without this new family. I don't know how such grace was bestowed. After my vision of knowing when I first met Barbara, I looked in her eyes and saw someone that I could deeply trust. This was a revelation. We never fell into a clinch of romantic love. We chose to be partners and began the long dance. It hasn't always been easy, but in those difficult moments I let the mystery of my vision about our relationship master my fears and desires. I met my daughter when she was five and I simply knew that I wanted to be her father. I remember with clarity and feeling the moment when I said goodnight and she first called me Dad. We have all stood atop Moro Rock together in the summer and we have skied through the snow draped cinnamon sequoias in the midst of winter white. Someday I will take them deep into the backcountry of the Great Western Divide. Without them this story would have ended years ago, this fire before us never lit.

I love to cross-country ski the winter landscape, especially in a light storm or soon after. The landscape takes on a more primal feel and makes it easier to sustain who I really am. There is only the sound of the skis gliding with each forward kick and thrust, accompanied by the sporadic sounds of a few animals braving the snowy day. Each year I take some of my students to ski the high country above Yosemite. On the last day we ski to the overlook at Dewey Point directly opposite El Capitan. My hope is that even one of the students will sense something of the mystery in the view and take it with them.

The last time we were in Yosemite I again took the students to the point. After I checked the cornice of snow for safety I invited students to come out with me and take in the view. Some students sat with their lunches and chose not to take it all in. Maybe they were bored or maybe they were afraid of taking it all in. Sometimes a vision can knock you off your cherished beliefs of what life is. Maybe they wanted things to remain exactly as they were and wanted nothing to disturb that. As we skied down the trail back to the rental center I could feel the rhythm of my motion, the kick and the extended glide. Around me I could see some of the kids starting to feel their own rhythm even as they skied uphill. When we walked into the rental center to check in our skis the radio detailed the beginning of the bombing of Iraq. I looked around sadly. In a world of countless vistas, there was no vision to be had. Everyone had feared to really see, feared to embrace the difference of another way, feared that they would be knocked off their cherished beliefs. Money and cleverness compounded by fear had once again overwhelmed the real seeing, the real knowledge of what needed to be done.

A year after I first stood on top of Moro Rock I returned to enter the backcountry. I began the journey the day after the autumnal equinox when the days and nights, the light and the dark, are of equal length. As I passed Moro Rock, I imagined Robert Johnson being there on my return and I would be able to tell him what I had seen. I put on my old boots which no longer fit quite right and shouldered a borrowed pack. I was returning to the High Sierra after more than a ten-year absence.

The High Sierra Trail starts at Crescent Meadow and winds across the granite peaks and valleys to its end at Mt. Whitney. It curves through a dense forest to the southeast of Crescent Meadow and suddenly emerges on the edge of the Canyon of the Middle Fork. To the rear, Moro Rock protrudes with the ridges falling away to the San Joaquin Valley. Across the canyon, The Undertakers stand guard to secrets of the Grail. I stepped forth with my old boots and an ill fitting pack weighed down by things unseen, my spirit compressed by the insults and fears of life as we live it. I was leaving behind the stories of the Great Valley, hoping to find something new.

I find myself under a massive weight that seems like a forty-foot cube. A dark man who is keeping to the shadows is lowering it on to me. I cannot see his face. I

am lying on my back and the great weight presses my chest so that I can hardly breathe. The man says that he will release the weight when I know that I can take it no longer. I feel like I am dying. I awake with a start and gasp for breath.

Mehrten Creek

Imagine if you can Whatever It Was (and Is), the nothing that becomes something. As the something brought more and more of itself into existence it became stars and planets, oceans, mountains and microbes. Then came all of those creatures that could dream. Whatever It Was now had a voice, a neural net of sparkling images, even though it couldn't speak. Bison and great cats, mammoth and gazelle moved from the created world into the net of the great mind and back in a quicksilver salmon rush of energy. In the cyclical nighttime journey from the high mountain source to the sea and back, from the created to the uncreated the people had a way to Know. The landscape was the mind, the day and the night partners in knowing, threaded together by a silver current.

Are your days and nights partners in some sort of spiritual equinox? Are they linked by some unknown energy of cooperation? Do they live to serve each other with some semblance of reverence? Does your night wake to greet the day, your day slip thankfully into the night? This is the great harmony.

The Energy comes from the deep recesses of the night. If the day does not carry out the real vision of the night, then there is a great damming of the flow, a building pressure of insanity. My friend the medicine man once explained how he was chosen for his work. Each year the Elders chose the children who showed the greatest inner Energy and for twelve years taught them how to use this force for the benefit of the people. He also told me how if a child had this Energy and was not trained, that a craziness would engulf them as an adult. I pictured how the Energy would ricochet around inside the body like a bullet in a steel drum. I remembered myself as a child bouncing off the walls that I couldn't see, a pot pulled over my head like I was a knight blinded by my armor, jousting with unknown forces. A piece of me broke when he told me this for I had a sense of knowing something indefinable in my first five years, of having no Elder to aid in my birth and, like my sister, breathing too soon the air of another reality and living in my own shit, alone, afraid and untutored.

I look around and find myself in a dark room with an exit door shaped like a vagina. Suddenly I'm standing at the back of a crowd that has gathered outside the door and I know that inside is a small black child. I hear talk among the people as they plot to quickly jerk the child through the door before its time; they hope that it will breathe too soon and intend to watch it die.

I turn and walk into a nearby courtroom where the child is being tried. As the proceedings continue I am the only one to rise to the child's defense. I know that the jurors are prejudiced against this black child of the darkness and so I speak emphatically and passionately about what I see as their deep-rooted prejudice and the need for love in this situation.

I can see that no one has heard me as the jurors
prepare to pass sentence. I leave the courtroom quickly
and find a place where no one can see me, grab a
sharp blade, then cut and create an opening to the
womb room. I beckon the child to me, gather him up
and take him to safety.

As I emerged from the forest surrounding Crescent Meadow I looked down and across the canyon of the Middle Fork. Below me were the blackened traces of an old fire that swept through the area. A sign along the trail noted that it was called the Buckeye Fire. It had started below on the river and burned uphill to the edge of the Sequoia giants, fueled by the accumulation of decades of unburned debris. When the pioneers reached the Sierra they marveled at the openness of the forest as opposed to the dense undergrowth of the forests of the East. Fires naturally burned through the low growth periodically, but never grew large enough to reach up into the trees themselves. Suppression of the energy of fire had changed all of that.

I followed the edge of the canyon for a short while and then turned away through the forest. The forest became dark, so choked with fallen branches and deadfalls that I felt as if I was walking through a time bomb that could explode around me at any moment. It reminded me of our collective mind, our common mind that has been ignored for so long, debris laden, dark and foreboding. Each of us has to remove our own portion of the dark unclaimed debris, perform our own individual fuel reduction, before the fire can safely burn through in its cycles and keep things clear.

The forest was gloomily silent around me, the ground covered with the lifeless tree carcasses. My goal was to get to Mehrten Creek to camp for the evening, but I had no idea what it looked like or what to expect. I did hope for something special. As I crossed the many branches of Panther Creek that flowed through the deadened forest, I wondered at each small crossing if this could be Mehrten Creek. With a sudden crashing sound a honey-yellow bear bolted across the trail in front of me, hurtled on down the mountainside at high speed, followed by the descent of silence once again. Not even a bird sound broke through the heavy veil.

That dark and debris laden forest reminded me of the depression that has afflicted me at times in my life and of what it felt like to suppress my own instincts and energies in order to survive the circumstances of my life. Numbness is a survival tactic. The emptiness and echoing silence was a reminder of growing up with no one to talk to about the true nature of things and having to walk through a lifescape populated by those who were spiritually dead or ignorant.

In contrast I find myself alive when I am visited by the energy of the spirits, when Whatever It Was (and Is) dons its cloak of the many symbols that bridge the worlds and comes to me. I have remodeled our once featureless tract house from one end to the other with my own hands in order to create a place for these spirits to call home. The yard has been landscaped, the lawn gone, so that Crow will be attracted to land in the tree and know that this is the right place to leave its noisy message. Whatever It Was (and Is) will dwell with me if I build a suitable place for it to live.

When I look out over the Great Valley, I dream of restoring it to a place the spirits could call home, of restoring the oak forests of the valley floor, of restoring Tulare Lake and the multiple strands of life that once teemed there. We have to make some positive gestures of sincerity to that of which we are created. If I lay a brick, God lays a brick, like the transcontinental railway built from opposite ends. Vision guides the survey till the rails are met with a golden spike. I dream of the land of my birth being restored and the people calling to Whatever It Was (and Is) and saying, "We now see. We are ready, come home to us." I dream of the spirits coming home to Dutch Bill and my ancestors, of the voices that whispered in the spring at Dumtah finally speaking through this story. This is the real Ghost Dance.

What does your home reflect, what does your life reflect? Are they places for the spirits to dwell? In my darkest times I have still built my house and planted my yard in welcome. What do you do in your dark times? That is why we are sitting here, trying to find that sustaining vision which will carry us into the day. I'll say this. Keep to your vision. Keep building, keep restoring that which has been dammed or drained or defiled, no matter what. Do everything with craft and intent. Like in Exeter, my old hometown, paint murals in your life even if you feel dark and afraid. Revision and restore your landscape to begin to change your mind. Even if we are not yet whole we can begin to restore things until the moment that we become whole. And then we can continue to revision and restore things.

Clarence King was plagued by a melancholy his entire life, as if nothing that he did was ever enough. Nothing could dispel his inheritance of loss. He still pursued his grail of being the first man atop Mt. Whitney. In 1871 he left his survey party in Wyoming to make a trip to San Francisco. On his return to Wyoming he made a detour to Lone Pine in the Owens Valley, because the image of Whitney still burned in his mind. King caught a stagecoach in Carson City for the 280-mile trip south along the rift valley along the eastern side of the Sierra.

When he arrived he had to wait two days for a storm to clear. When the sun rose on the massive granite uplift that is the Eastern Sierra, King set out with a hired companion to finally attain his goal. As they neared the top they had to make their way through the rock and ice debris left by the passage of old avalanches. Finally at the top King could survey the grand expanse from the summit of his goal. To the west at the bottom of the canyon lay the Kern River, and beyond, the Kaweah Peaks, while to the north Mt. Brewer protruded above Kings Canyon. He could also see to the north the east-west range of peaks that formed the Kern-Kings Divide where he had crossed years before. To the east was the desert expanse of the White Mountains and beyond them Death Valley. After a while King and his partner descended into the clouds, scarcely able to see, the wind howling.

For two years King was hailed as the conqueror of Mt. Whitney, then it was discovered that he had climbed the wrong mountain. He had climbed Mt. Langley six miles to the south.

A goal is a strange thing. What does it mean to attain it? Does life instantly change, does it quiet the demon, flesh out the face of the Living Dead or is it just cleverness at high altitude? Is there completeness, the fractured pieces coming to one? We can feel whole on the peaks and fall apart in the valleys. How does the vision extend into the marshes and bogs of life?

Dear John,

I am happy with your letter and I am happy with you.

Yes, we can talk about the progress of your life and I hope I can help. You are a good man and we can start from that.

My first advice to you is something that you can't possibly understand or assimilate now. It would be too great a shock to your youthful system and might even do damage. But store it away and claim it later when you have the power to accept it.

You are *already* the noble man you wish to be; you are a complete human being, a very fine one and there is nothing that you have to earn and no hurdles to jump to claim your genius. If you could see yourself as I see you, you would be so pleased and so happy that you would glow for a week. The act of being, which you are, is complete and it needs nothing more. True, there are lots of things for you to do and the rest of your life is hardly enough time to accomplish what you will do; but the *you-ness*, which is the essential you is already there, complete, finished, functioning, creative. This is an act of being and has nothing to do with what you do. Of course you will do things, but that is far down the list of virtues of your life. What you are is already functional and has nothing to do with what you have earned or anything else in the competitive world. It is to that part of you that I spoke in Santa Barbara. You heard and have been knocked out of your old orbit by it, but not quite yet into a new orbit. You have heard but do not believe. That is what has to come later and you must store this away until you can bear it. Keep it as a treasure and don't let *anything* damage it. It is your most precious possession. Don't let any depression or doubt erode it away.

Yes, there are lots of practical things to think about. What mark will you make in the world? What additional training will you do? What study is in your capacity? What relationships belong to you? All these are good and noble things—though they do not have one small damn thing to do with your worth and value. As above, this is already established.

You will batter about, feeling good one day, bad another day, success one time, failure another time because you can't hold the noble vision of yourself which is already you. I have to hold that gold for you for a while until you can bear it yourself. I do this with great pleasure because I believe in you.

All right, noble man, here is your face shown to you—straight and without editing. Please take it as soon as you can and keep faith and courage in the meantime.

Please have my faith and respect in you,

Robert

Mehrten Creek cascades down a steeply tilting rock face of exfoliating granite, the water sparkling in the light. The western edge threads its way through the forest edge while the eastern edge spreads itself over the wide exposed granite face in a lacework of rills and sheeting flows. Suddenly I realized that this great beauty was all mine, a legacy that I had never known.

I had entered camp in the evening enshrouded in dense clouds that pierced me with dampness and cold. The night was spent restless next to the murmuring stream, the temperature in the midthirties. I arose to sunlight and a thicket of wild raspberries next to my tent. Across the canyon, Castle Rocks thrust outward and upward, looming, glistening in the morning sun that arose over the Great Western Divide. Mehrten Creek seemed to point directly to the castle's core, The Undertakers ready to guide me on the trail.

I'm at the head of a group of people as we move on foot across a wooded valley and then up a wide trail through the forest that leads directly up the mountain on the other side. I begin to run, even though I'm barefoot and wearing my practice gi and hakama. As I run I feel joy and with every running stride up the mountain I rise a foot into the air. At the top of the mountain I playfully run large circles in the air as I wait for the others.

Bearpaw

Sometimes we ceaselessly keep on roaming and never stop to figure out where we are. We are stopped for the moment, right here and now, where we sit at this fire. Sometimes the act of searching becomes an end in itself.

"Who are you?"

"I'm a seeker."

"When do you become a finder?"

Sometimes along the road our search begins to go around in endless circles constantly covering the same ground. Some of these circles we call churches or philosophies or addictions. I'm no stranger to spinning these spiritual circles.

I lived in a yoga ashram once on the East Coast in my late twenties. I agonized for months about whether to officially commit myself to life there, to give up my old name and take a new Sanskrit name. I tried to picture life at the ashram in its regimented detail extending into an indefinite future. I remembered the freedom of the Sierra and thought of how I might be leaving that landscape behind.

Sometimes the ashram would have special weekends with outside guests. As I guided them through the grounds the guests voiced envy about my living in such a spiritual place.

Their envy and their unquestioned acceptance of this strange spiritual path made me feel better about my choice. I was a missionary of sorts and helping to make converts was a way to ease my own doubts. I suspect that this lies at the heart of missionaryism, that missionaries are really trying to convince themselves of the validity of what they believe. Every convert eases doubts and keeps the missionary on their unexamined path.

I finally decided to make the commitment and was given a Sanskrit name. But the internal struggle took a toll and I hadn't realized the power that dwelt in my family name, and that it couldn't be given up lightly. Like a demon the name carried a contorted face, but behind the face dwelt the seeds of knowledge and wholeness. Once again my gut gave out and I ended up in the hospital.

I returned to the ashram to recuperate. I awoke one morning as all the others were off doing yoga and chanting. The guru stood at the foot of my bed, spread his arms and laid himself over me, then merged. I awoke from the dream within the dream. I had no idea who to talk to about all of this. What could it mean? I really wanted to be in the guru's favor. Did this mean that somehow I was chosen? I wanted to believe that.

What I didn't realize at the time was that the guru was being relocated from outside myself to within. I was being asked to trust my own instincts without having to be validated, without someone else telling me what to do. I had always lived my life seeking the approval of others and now the center of power in my life was trying to relocate to some deeper internal place. When I realized with great clarity that it was time to leave the ashram I was asked to meet with the guru. As we sat opposite each other with our legs folded on the floor he said, "Madhuvan, when you make important decisions like this, you are supposed to consult your guru." For the first time in my life I knew I already had.

The relocation of power, though, created more Energy than I could bear without guidance. I found that I didn't trust the guru to tell me the unvarnished truth and I didn't know where to turn. As usual I was left with no one to talk to, no mentor without agenda or scriptures.

Every evening we wore white and danced and chanted while the guru played the harmonium in the incense-scented air. I wondered, "Why chanting, why white?" and "Why do teachers have to play the harmonium?" Is this what I would have to do for the rest of my life in order to see and to continue to see? I didn't see the point of adopting an alien culture when I didn't fully understand my own.

I once stood up in the middle of a service and asked the guru, "Why all this?" as my hand swept around the room to the white clad worshippers, the incense, the harmonium and the chanting. Was all of this necessary to communicate with whatever we thought was God? His reply was, "I don't need this, but they do." Why do we need all of that? Why don't we just stop and see instead of remaining in subjugation? The guru was wrong, though. He did need all of that. He needed it for his own job security.

My best friend had moved to the ashram before I arrived. On my arrival he told me a story. A man had decided to seek enlightenment so he climbed into the high mountains to find an appropriate cave. He lived there for twenty years while doing various penances and ascetic practices, counting his prayer beads, chanting and praying. At the end of that time he attained enlightenment, so he decided to go back to his old village to display his new state of mastery and being. As he walked through the busy market square of farmers selling their fruits and seeds, of peddlers selling all possible manner of things, someone stepped on his foot. The master hit him.

He was master of one world, but not all, a still fractured existence.

When I decided to leave the ashram I was busy building furniture from walnut and spalted maple, cherry and oak, for the guru's guru who was coming from India. He was considered an enlightened master who came along only once every five hundred years. Someone asked how it felt to be making furniture for God. I replied, "Like I was making furniture for you."

On the day he arrived I had been working for twenty-four hours to finish my tasks. I walked to where he was being greeted and was bestowing his blessings. I saw a balding pudgy man with a baby's simple expression being waited on hand and foot. He knew little or nothing of dealing with the teeming marketplace, of the process of growing fresh fruit and other foods, of pruning and shaping trees, of gluing and shaping wood, less yet of the mystery of the Sierra. I knew a lot about helpless feelings and of wanting people to take care of me. I knew little of the fullness of life, of vigor and choice. I walked away and got into my truck without a word, drove away in my exhaustion. I was headed back to where the landscape matched the whorls and ridges of my mind.

As I prepared to leave Mehrten Creek I looked around the campsite at the surrounding pine and juniper, a single blue spruce jutting out in camp. A solitary hummingbird fed on a penstemon that protruded from a crack in the granite by the stream. Dark red manzanita wound through the boulders. I could take in all of this beauty intellectually but some barrier existed within that prevented me from directly feeling and sensing this place.

As I left the area around Mehrten Creek I entered forests that once again closed around me. Suddenly the trail opened to ledges blasted out of the solid granite wall. The stone mountain fell away sharply toward the Middle Fork of the Kaweah as it traced its way through the canyon below, the riverbed slowly rising toward the trail as I moved along. To the rear, the tip of Moro Rock was becoming a small punctuation point on the horizon, the view dominated by Castle Rocks. Views of Sugarbowl Dome and Little Blue Dome emerged along the trail before me.

As I walked I could feel the discomfort of my pack. My old trusty pack had a gotten a tear in it, so Barbara had handed me this one and wanted me to take it on the trip. I guess I felt I should take some load of hers with me on this quest, though I decided I would never wear this pack again. At times hiking felt more like plodding as I labored beneath the weight of my being. Shrubs of ripened bitter cherries began to appear along the trail, and all along the ground were mounds of red stained bear scat, cherry stones protruding in every direction.

I arrived in Bearpaw Meadow between 1:30 and 2:00 in the afternoon. The camp was like a small deserted city. During the summer the entire campground is full, with tent cabins across the meadow, a horse-packing mecca. Soon the sky began to close in again, the clouds moving across the valley from the barely visible Great Western Divide. The clouds soon engulfed the camp as the temperature dropped and the moist chill began to work my bones. The camp was vast with paths lined everywhere with logs. I felt as if I could get lost in the place. Seeing a large mound of rocks near the center of the deserted camp I decided to pitch my tent there. I seemed to be the only human body in a city of spirits and I kept listening for voices.

I lit a campfire around 5:00 to create some warmth and sense of company, but soon the old depression and melancholy began to descend on me like a shroud. The old dark questions welled up from the deep. How could I ever be happy, how could life ever finally work for me, how could this crazy journey possibly change my life? I had been plodding, one foot in front of the other, with a heavy uncomfortable pack and nothing felt like it was changing. It seemed like a reenactment of my entire life.

I don't know what I had really wanted to find. Maybe I wanted to just wake up happy and stay that way. Maybe some great being would spring from behind a rock and show me the mysteries of the universe. I suddenly heard what I thought was a voice down near the latrine, but it was only a raven flying through the echoing camp, laughing.

For a long time after I left the ashram I didn't want to get near spiritual teachers, but in the midst of depression and my mismanaged energy I decided to visit a nearby Zen center. As I was being given instruction in Zen sitting, the light came through the translucent rice paper shoji screens in a just-so fashion. I felt as if I had been in that place many times before. For the moment I felt a wave of peace. Over the next few years

I attended a few *sesshins*, or meditation sessions, and did a little work. At a *dokusan*, an interview with the roshi, he said to me, "When I saw you I said to myself, here comes John Spivey and his story." I might have replied, "Here is Roshi and his old Buddhist story," but didn't.

I felt empty and not in a good Buddhist sense. I was looking for someone to help me understand this story and I suddenly knew that Roshi couldn't do it. He might have looked at me with compassion, but he couldn't touch me with love. Compassion is rooted in sadness at the state of existence. Real love is rooted in the joy of extending one's life force to touch another, joy at being full of the process of life. I knew that there was some power at the core of the story that I couldn't dismiss, even to be a Buddha. Buddhists always speak of the inherent emptiness of phenomena and the Buddha's compassion. They don't really talk of love. I was looking for a sense of fullness, a sense that being alive was not a sin or cosmic joke, an illusion to be overcome.

I stoked the fire and waited to see what would join me. Two does crossed from right to left about one hundred feet in front of me to forage for a while. They edged closer as we eyed each other, till they slowly walked away, their white butts gleaming in the firelight and near darkness.

Suddenly I was startled by a cough to my right. A medium large black bear began to walk in my direction. I eyed the bear for a moment with *ki*, and he slowly ambled away. As I went to sleep I thought I heard voices echoing unintelligibly across the meadow like hallucinations or feverish dark thoughts. I had been told that I was a complete human being, but I couldn't grasp that reality. It was a vision that I had not digested and taken into my heart and bone marrow. Instead I was constantly sliding down that crack in the ground to avoid facing knowing.

Valhalla

As you sit here at this fire, are you all of one piece, or are you scattered in myriad pieces over time and space, scattered like the debris of ten thousand random collisions? Do you even know the difference?

What does it mean to be all of one piece? Are there holes in your being where you know that something inexplicable belongs? Occasionally all of the pieces randomly align in a moment of clarity and then suddenly the moment is gone. Sometimes on a high mountain, stress and danger can force the pieces together into that clear moment and again it's gone. People climb higher and higher peaks to get back to a sense of being all of one piece.

I simply climb peaks to get a view of where all the pieces lie. It's difficult to round up all of the fragments; it's akin to herding ten thousand wild cattle on your own. Better to see where they are, find a seat in their middle and let them come home to you. But who is the *you* that they come home to?

This coming together is available anywhere, but it takes courage and self-discipline to get there. Self-discipline has the image of being sackcloth and ashes, of being rigidly humorless. It's nothing more than understanding what truly needs to be done in any given moment and doing it. Yet how do we know what truly needs to be done?

Let's talk about living in the moment. Some people think that living in the moment means responding to any and every impulse. First impulse, best impulse. But tell me this, who is it that is having the impulse, your true self or one of the many fractured pieces? Can you know the difference? Truly being in the moment embraces all time and all place gathered into the true self. Living in the moment bows to the ancestors and respects the generations to come. Being in true self, one just knows what to do. It is beyond impulse and desire.

When I began to study the martial art of Aikido my first teacher would tell me of his trips to Japan to study with his teacher there, one of the original students of the founder. After hard practice every day, they would go to drink sake. Each night my teacher would have to help carry his teacher home. The Aikido master knew what needed to be done in practice on the mat but didn't know what truly needed to be done off the mat. I have wondered why, if we work so hard to polish the mirror of mind to crystal clarity, we choose to fog, obscure and deface what we have created. Can we know the needs of all moments, not just ones on the mat or in the mountains? A good student has to come to know off-the-mat mind.

The study of Aikido is meant to unify the body and the mind into a one pieceness of being. I received my black belt from a teacher who bedeviled me. He was on old Japanese man who had been beaten by his father and also interred in the American concentration camp at Manzanar, not far from the base of Mt. Whitney on the eastern side of the Sierra. He seemed to feel that he had to make my life harder in order to teach me something, as if my life had not been hard enough. I was always told what I was doing wrong, but never what I was doing right.

He was trying to teach us unification of body and mind, but he didn't realize how many parts of himself were spread across the landscape, from Japan to Santa Barbara to Manzanar. Despite this I consciously chose to stay and become a *shodan* because I knew that getting a black belt was the right thing to do. I really wanted a teacher to communicate with about the deeper things in my life, yet this was all I had. I was belittled and shamed but I kept moving forward because of my love of the art.

I dreamed of being good enough to go to Japan and study, and then I found out that the politics at the top were not much different than the politics at the bottom. Progress at the top was determined by unquestioned obedience to the head *sensei* and obedience to tradition, with no regard given to teaching students how to know for themselves. The founder of Aikido had created the discipline as a path to enlightenment. But when he died, his chief students, in feudal fashion, divvied up the art into small fiefdoms. The founder had fostered Aikido as an expression of love, but no one seems to understand the depth of his concept any longer. Love is not a samurai concept. The urge toward hierarchy has triumphed over spiritual knowledge. Most schemes of hierarchy promote greater levels of cleverness as one moves to the top as well as greater commitment to the hierarchy. More intricate cleverness, more clever cleverness.

Nearly thirty years ago I stood on a bluff overlooking the gentle undulations of the Eel River. The Eel is one of Northern

California's rivers that still hosts the wild rush of spawning salmon and steelhead. Below me the river was lined with sand and jumbled rock. Around me pastures stretched toward a sparse forest. It was many miles from any town. I was there for a meditation retreat with a noted Buddhist teacher. I had read one of his books and been impressed by it.

One of his students told me that this was a rather uneventful retreat, that normally the students would be tent hopping in various sexual couplings and drinking till late at night. All of this was in emulation of their teacher and their notion of living in the moment. As I looked around the landscape from my vantage on the bluff, I began to see all of us who were there as cattle that simply switched one fenced pasture for another. I knew that the truth lay all around me in the landscape and in the river that housed the silver current. Above me in a house on the hillside, devoted students were meditating and chanting to find something. I could pull at the edges of understanding this view, but I couldn't quite absorb it all. Meanwhile, Buddha was all around me.

Many years later the teacher died, yellow and jaundiced, liver eaten away from alcohol, despite his self-proclaimed diamond body. Students still follow him. I think we excuse teachers far too easily because we are always looking for ways to excuse ourselves. Sometimes I challenge my students to try and make it through the day without making a single excuse. It is usually the hardest thing that they have ever done. The mountain cares nothing for excuses.

I have high standards for teachers. One shouldn't talk about what one cannot manifest. It terribly confuses the people and distorts the very meaning of why we are here on this planet. Humans don't learn much from words and speeches and sermons. They learn by watching and studying. Walking the road is more profound than talking. If I want to climb Mt. Whitney and I find a sign that points in that direction, then that is a vision. If I don't walk in that direction the vision is useless. If a teacher says that they have seen a sign somewhere pointing toward Mt. Whitney, but they are not walking steadily in that direction, then what they say is only a rumor of the truth and is worse than meaningless, it is shit along the trail.

I make no excuses for myself. I have done things in my past of which I am ashamed. There were reasons, but reasons don't constitute an excuse. I hope that somehow I can be forgiven. Things are different now, times are different. Something greater than my past failure wells up around me and within me. I have no diamond body. My body is made of muscle and sinew, protoplasm and organs, a pulsating heart and blood, red with hemoglobin, red with iron from the furnace of stars.

Can you look your failures and shortcomings in the eye without excuse, learn and move on? Defog, clean and polish the mirror, "Go and sin no more."

About 7:30 in the morning the sun finally rose over Kaweah Gap in the east. The sun's rays slowly crept down to illuminate the boulder pile where I was camped. In the light I could finally see several tents down by the meadow. A woman camper with long gray hair pulled back in a braid walked by, but with no sign of acknowledgement. I felt invisible in the background emptiness of the campground. The sound of a helicopter began to pulse across the sky. I watched as it circled around a peak and began to bear down on the meadow and finally landed on a grassy knoll on the other side. The knoll had been indiscernible from where I stood because the meadow greenery of mule's ear, corn lilies and ferns had hidden all of the contours of the ground.

I packed my gear, circled my campsite in a final sweep and hefted my pack. The pack suddenly felt better and my spirits buoyed. I had to walk back uphill to go around the upper end of the meadow to get to the main trail. Before I hit the main trail the helicopter fired up again as the pilot waved a greeting to me. I turned right at the trail junction just as the helicopter lifted off, the rotor wash flattening the meadow and pushing a breeze past me. The trail flattened and with it came a sense of ease.

The trail widened by an A-frame ranger station where four or five young people were taking down tent cabins for the season. One of the young women waved at me as a plaintive rock and roll song issued from a tape deck. I suddenly felt a robustness for the youth and rock and roll energy of this camp and trail maintenance crew. For a moment I considered this trail crew life in the High Sierra, its vigor and physical appeal. With a sudden hearty laugh to myself, I thought, "I'm getting too old for that shit," and remembered my relatively new family at home and the new worldview it offered me. There were still some trails that I wanted to blaze, though, both in and out of the mountains.

After discussions with Tibetan Buddhists, Timothy Leary was reputed to have said that LSD and the Buddhist spiritual path led to the same place. LSD was like a helicopter that could fly to the same peak that devotees reached by walking the trail. That is only true if the peak is a goal. When you walk along the trail you can observe all of the nuances of life along the way, the lizards, the marmots, the tracks and scat of bear and the nature of lichen on the rocks. All of this is lost in the rush to the top. We long to fly, but there is much to be learned from walking the dusty road. The mountain peak is a direction for movement, but not a goal.

When Clarence King found out that he had climbed the wrong peak, he hurried back to the Owens Valley to make it right. When he finally made it to the top on September 19, 1873, he was a month too late. His was the fourth party to make it to the top. Three fishermen had made it to the summit first, so Mt. Whitney was christened Fishermen's Peak for a period of time. King had lost the distinction of being the first to the goal and also missed out on much along the trail.

A few yards past the cabins the view suddenly opened up across River Canyon to the looming presence of Eagle Scout Peak across the gorge. Far back down the canyon I could still see the Undertakers standing guard. The trail wound through stands of various conifers and then opened to expanses of manzanita and even larger views of River Valley. At that moment I realized that this expanse was what I had come for. I could feel my spirit begin to lift even more.

The trail moved on through stands of black oak followed by steep slopes covered with fern, wild raspberry and a profusion of Indian paintbrush. As I walked along the trail it became a pathway etched into the granite canyon wall where rills and rivulets tumbled across it, then down the mountainside to the Kaweah a thousand feet below. Across the canyon the scooped out granite face of Eagle Scout Peak formed a great steep bowl and chute where boulders had tumbled down the mountainside. A small stream of water cascaded down the bowl and then on down the chute, glistening in the morning light.

The trail and the greenery above it seemed supported by immense fractures of granite slabs that trailed down the mountainside. Above the trail the trees thinned to lone stands holding out in the midst of the granite. Soon the trail dipped into a V-shaped notch that ran down the mountainside straight to the Kaweah. In the notch a stone bridge forded a small stream. All around were indications of the torrent that had come down this way during the spring and early summer. Around the corner from the bridge the trail came out on a promontory with immense views from Kaweah Gap down to Castle Rocks. I dropped my pack to sit on a boulder and write. A charcoal grey, almost black, blue bellied lizard watched me all the while, his tail lost somewhere out in the food chain. A chill breeze blew up the canyon.

The view made me stop and think of my artist friend Davis and his ability to depict all that this landscape had to communicate. For years we shared my shop and talked about the deep things as we built different constructions of wood. His lithographs hang on walls all over the house where I live in Santa Barbara. Once a woman sat through an all-day meeting in the living room and throughout the day I could see her looking mesmerized at two of the lithographs on the wall. One was of a great ancient, gnarled oak tree, the other of a desert boulder field in Baja, both rendered in great depths of detail. Somehow Davis has mastered the ability to intimate the existence of another world on the other side of this reality. His art exists as a door to be entered and the woman felt compelled to enter as if into a shaman's world. His skill is great, yet it is not clever. More importantly his understanding is great. His work conveys something about the deep, dark and mysterious nature of things. I hope that my words can convey as much.

As I set out on the trail I kept stopping in awe to marvel at the views. I rounded a bend and caught a quick view of a white granite tower called Angel Wings. A sense of being in the realm of the sacred began to overtake me. I turned yet another bend and could look back to a view of an immense granite outcropping that was narrower at the bottom and then ascended outward and rounded into a dome. I longed for Davis to be with me to record the view and so that we could laugh, sip tea and point at rocks and trees in delight. There are times to be alone, but there is also much to share on the trail. There are times to sit and just be, mind-to-mind.

The trail began to traverse the sides of several exfoliating domes, their onionskins sloughing off all around me, the trail a blasted groove in the rounded faces. The trail began to descend through manzanita, black oak and wildflowers to meet Lone Pine Creek. The creek was a tumult of boulders and pools, the water icy clear. I began to feel as if the water was becoming clear enough to truly wash something dirty from my soul. Every step now seemed to carry me further into the vision.

At the far side of the bridge across the creek I sat on a granite stairstep to write a little more. As I wrote I heard a sound behind me and turned to greet a man and a twelve-year-old boy. We began an exchange. As we talked I learned that they were from Bakersfield where the Kern River comes to its murky dead end. We traded stories of backcountry perils, of near misses with storms and hypothermia and how lucky we were as dumb beginners when no one had properly taught us how to be in these places. He said that he hadn't gone as far as he had planned because his son had hurt his ankle and wasn't up to the full journey. I replied that when you take your kids into the mountains, it's no longer your trip, it's theirs, and you have to teach them about how to be here in this place. He agreed this was true, that he didn't want to push him and disillusion him. We said goodbye as they headed off to a different alpine lake at the head of Lone Pine Creek to try their hand at fishing.

From Lone Pine Creek the trail ascended steeply and I began to feel my legs and pack again. Once more I encountered stretches of trail where it had been blasted out of the granite, traces of drill holes for the dynamite still visible in the monolith of stone. As I looked for a good spot to rest I saw a lone pine tree growing from a slight bulge in the trail. A blue jay screeched from the tree to draw me onward.

The trail wound up, down and around, barely letting me keep whatever precious altitude I had gained. The trailside was once more covered by granite and manzanita where lizards constantly ran out onto the trail to challenge me. I stopped to observe one as he puffed himself up in challenge, his throat and belly swelling in a distended blue. Furiously he did a few pushups to test my mettle, but I didn't take the challenge. I just stood still and watched as he gradually began to relax. It was as if all the lizards were guarding the way for their brother snake, guardian of all things subterranean and dark. Who goes and why? They stood guard over entry into the dark reptilian recesses of the brain.

Our brain lies in layers folded around an ancient core. The

layers mark our growth through the evolution of the shape and form of our bodies, of the evolution of our being here. At the center of the brain is a reptile's brain and at its center, a place that knows only the presence and absence of fear. If you see violence being done, this core place sees only the violence as if it were happening to you. This place is so dark and primeval that it doesn't know the difference between illusion and reality. There is only violence and fear as it if it were happening to you. All violence happens to you. We now choose to witness violence for pleasure, whether real or illusion, on the screen. The dark place knows no difference. It is always happening to you. We toy with this place in ourselves like playing with our genitals. We play with the adrenaline rush of fear to wake us from our emptiness and dying. The center of the brain twists and contorts in this self-induced adrenal pain and fear as we struggle to pleasure ourselves and feel alive. The circuits of my body have been burned out by the adrenaline of the fear of living. I choose to not induce more fear upon my being, to not induce more twisting living death. Exploring the deeper reason and finding a deeper joy can heal the circuits of the body and the mind.

The reptilian challenge caused me to stop and recall why I was on this particular path. More and more lizards ran out to take a quick look at me as I started to walk, then moved back from the trail as if to allow passage.

As I moved on I could see water tumbling down a rounded granite face ahead. The trail ascended once more for a long stretch then switched back to reveal pools of water at the top of the falls that I had just spotted. I jumped over and waded across the pools, struck with a keen pleasure at this place. I walked over to the edge of the falls to peer at where the cascade plunged downward on its run to the Kaweah. I had arrived at Hamilton Creek. James Hamilton, the explorer and namesake of this place, had married one of the Mehrten women and so was part of our family pantheon. Dutch Bill and other family members are buried in the Hamilton Cemetery.

I turned around to look upstream when suddenly I was overwhelmed with the massive white granite Angel Wings soaring over me. It had been hidden from view on the trail to the pools. It leaped into my consciousness with the suddenness of seeing it so close for the first time. Angel Wings is a vertical sheer white face that rises above Hamilton Creek for perhaps two thousand feet, its face striated with vertical cracks that cross and interweave to give the appearance of feathers. I was struck with its majesty. It is what a gothic cathedral aspires to be, but never can.

The trail leading from the pools passed through dense underbrush of wild raspberries that threatened to choke off the trail. As I waded through the brush like a black bear I reached out to sample a few of the berries. I could feel within myself a simple gratitude for this lushness in such a high place.

The trail ascended steeply through the granite and once more I could feel the weight of my load both physically and spiritually. I knew that soon I would be able to set down my load at Upper Hamilton Lake. My plan was to camp there and day-hike to the top of Kaweah Gap. I was walking at the base of Angel Wings. It rose directly above me and as I craned my neck to see its summit the tower began to enfold me in awe. I am not much for this angel stuff. Where were they when I was so desperate as a child? A little glimpse or solace would have gone a long way. Something about these granite wings that soar in a monolith from the bowels of the earth toward the sky made me think of the angel of mercy. I also thought of Kanzeon or Kwan Yin, the Buddhist goddess of compassion. The whole granite massif, of which Angel Wings is a part, is called Valhalla, the abode of the gods.

I decided to stop above Little Hamilton Lake to drink water and write. A cicada whirred madly behind me and as I turned I could see it jump wildly into the air over and over. Below me the lake was cold and clear, deeply submerged rocks could be seen in crystal clarity from the trail a hundred feet above the water. I hoped that I too could become clear all of the way to the bottom, that all depths would be like one. The clouds began move up the gap and swirl around the granite tower. They also began to close in once more on me. I knew that I must push on for Upper Hamilton.

The Dream of the Depths

Have you ever examined what it means to be aware? Is it rigorously documenting the flora and fauna along the trail or knowing all of the constellations of the night sky? Or, is it something more?

In Aikido I sometimes practice *randori*, an exercise wherein three or four people attack me. At first there was only the blur of conflicting energies and collisions and of being finally overwhelmed by the attack. After much practice I became the center of the storm of swirling energies, calmly moving from place to place to deal with the attacks as they occurred. Aikido finally gave me a means to begin managing the wild flows of energy in my being, to begin to claim my real life from the beatings that I had taken.

Soon after I received my black belt I was driving north for the Christmas holidays in the midst of heavy traffic on a narrowed section of the highway. Suddenly a car entered from the side directly at me. The lane next to me was full, but in an instant I had maneuvered to my left and around the looming collision. I had no time to blow my horn, no time to get angry and curse. There was only direct action in the midst of the total is-ness. As I maneuvered I could feel the freedom of the moment, the total clarity. I felt like laughing in delight at the freedom from anger and the entry into a larger mind. Anger would have only slowed me down, perhaps been fatal. Clarity of action was faster and more profound than adrenaline. This is awareness. Very often we equate the rush of adrenaline with the sense of clarity, but it's only drugs, a helicopter to a false summit. If life is a freeway, then it's more important to focus on skillful driving than it is to focus on getting angry with the bad drivers.

I have told my students that they will probably never be physically attacked in their lives, but that they will attack themselves. Aikido, then, is really about dealing with this attack by our selves on our selves. In talking with an Aikido student who had been practicing for several years, I told him that he would know he was making headway in the art when he started to do Aikido in his dreams, when every attack by the demons in the night would be met in randori. Imagine turning to face the demon with a smile, happy to practice your newfound skill. You can never slay the demon, but you can do randori till it gives up its secret. Within randori there is no intent of violence, only perception of movement. There is a joy in these encounters when you can move beyond fear and anger, joy in the mastery of energy, joy in a movement within a larger mind. We may never be free from attack, but we can be free from fear.

You might say that I'm repressing something, but I'm not. All emotions are just energy. Movies show martial arts masters snatching flies from the air. This is nothing. Try instantaneously catching anger or fear from the air and sending its essence of energy through a different path, through a different neural circuit to feed the larger mind and the larger action. This is part of non-doing. This is alchemy. We defend our anger and our right to anger as if it were gold. The gold lies somewhere behind the anger and the fear.

Both of the Hamilton Lakes are glacially carved granite bowls beneath immense walls and peaks. Glacially scoured and polished granite slabs tilt down into Upper Hamilton. As I arrived, the clouds started to descend and shroud the upper peaks. My arrival was in mid-afternoon so I set up my tent in case of weather and then fixed an early dinner. I pitched the tent in a patch of decomposed granite, but several of the tent pegs refused to go down more than an inch because of the granite slab that lurked right beneath the surface. The trees all around the campsite were a type of fir, some standing erect; others were bent and broken by the weight of the winter storms into twisted spiraling shapes.

The campsite was near the outlet stream that cascaded from Upper Hamilton down to Lower Hamilton and by the foot of Angel Wings. The trail crosses the stream and begins its steep ascent to Kaweah Gap at the crest of the Great Western Divide. Across the lake I could see two ribbons of silver waterfalls plunging down the peaks into the bowl. As the clouds lowered the waterfalls seemed to fall from the mists and the sky. Angel Wings to the rear rose up into the clouds and disappeared. The white tower was standing on the granite heart of the Sierra, was part of the granite heart of the Sierra and was reaching up into the unseen. The tower pushed the mind to try and understand where it was that it pointed. The clouds began to lower even further so that at 4:00 in the afternoon it felt like twilight. I couldn't see more than one hundred to two hundred feet up the slopes around me and fifty to a hundred feet up the slopes across the lake.

I knew there would be no campfire at night to welcome and warm my thoughts and demons. Fires are prohibited and wood is scarce in the high realm of granite and water. Patches of snow still held out in shaded areas and gullies. I wondered what would come during the cloud enshrouded, moonless, fireless night in the middle of a boulder field above timberline. I would have to face my demons without the grace of fire. I bathed my tired and very dirty feet in the lake, a gesture of ablution to the spirits of the place. At 4:45 the opposite side of the lake became invisible.

With all of the moisture in the air the cold began to penetrate and I knew that the night would be close to freezing. The penetrating cold reminded me of the dank, cold tule fog on freezing mornings in the fields with my grandfather. There were no other campers anywhere near the lake and the engulfing clouds moved in wisps through the twisted trees to create an eerie and ghostly scene. Soon the visibility across the lake decreased to one hundred to two hundred feet and it seemed as if the lake depths could yield up almost anything to rise through the water and the fog. The world suddenly seemed full of the unknown.

As I sat to write I knew that coming to this place would change my life, but I did not know how. I thought of my family at home to whom I wanted to return with some new mastery in my life. I sat there with a pain in my belly which said that nothing I could ever do would be right, nothing I could ever do would be enough, a family legacy. The religion of my childhood had claimed that I was conceived in sin and born into sin, and I had little choice in the matter. I was condemned to hell long before I was born. It was a judgment handed through the generations and almost emblazoned in the DNA. Here at the headwaters of the family reality I wanted to go beyond the old judgments and find out who I really was. I wanted to understand why I could not take Robert's kind knowledge of me into my heart and bone marrow. As I wrote I began to shiver, even though I was well clothed against the cold. I longed for the comfort of fire. I would have to make my own.

I decided to do T'ai Chi and chose a spot on the gently descending smooth granite that angled down into the lake. I needed to generate the chi energy. I began my warm-ups and then moved into the form. Midway through the form the breath in the back of my throat began to take on the intensity of a camp stove. As I moved I began to notice that the granite beneath my feet was imbedded with black markings that looked like giant calligraphy. As I did "Wave Hands Like Clouds" I could see an island to my right that somehow had escaped my notice. Two lone white pine trees sprouted from the granite. The cloud mists folded around the island and the trees till it looked like a Chinese landscape painting. During "Fair Lady Works at Shuttles" I was surprised, as a large trout broke water out near the island, the only sound other than the outlet stream rippling on down the mountain toward Angel Wings.

I decided to try Chi Gong. As my palms faced outward near the end of the second round I could feel the energy and heat from them begin to push out to the reality around me. As I finished and looked at my hands and nails, I saw they had become bright red with energy and circulation. I looked out toward the island with the lone white pines once more and then looked downward to the magma folds in the granite at my feet. This entire landscape used to exist under miles of sediment beneath the ocean. With a sudden awareness, I realized that this truly was the dream of the depths thrust upward where it could clearly be seen. I was surrounded by the mystery. The surrounding dense fog was the descent of the clouds, meeting the earth and the depths right where I stood. For the moment all was met, the ocean depths, the mountains, the sky and myself. I could not read the calligraphic markings at my feet, but I knew their meaning. I was transported right back into the dream of the great fish. Again I was confronted with the vast sea bottom that sought expression, but this time it was as real as the granite beneath my feet. I knew that I was in this place for a reason. Take a pencil. Draw a picture of my face. Take it back home. I sat down to write, impelled by some force.

I went back to my tent as the mist thickened and darkness began to descend. As I sat in the tent and did ki breathing I could once more feel the heat begin to generate. I began to think again that I heard voices downstream, but it was only the outlet stream itself tumbling over the rocks. The sound of the stream as it flowed down toward the great valley far below seemed to contain the sound of all voices.

The mystery pressed closer and I could no longer see to write. I knew that somehow I had entered the Grail Castle. I had come to my source like a salmon swimming upstream. Would something old and outworn die in this place so that some new life could arise? Would I like Parsifal forget to remember the important question and be tossed out on my ear come morning? A voice seemed to say, "All shall be well and all manner of things shall be well." I sincerely hoped so. It would be a great sea change in the way that I imagined my life. Maybe there was real gold in these mountains, as the great White Chief had prophesied with the sweep of his hand.

Red Kaweah, Black Kaweah, Kaweah Queen

Some nights are so long and dark, cold and without fuel that you have to reach deep inside and strike a match. You become the fuel and the fire that illuminates the darkness. If you can find the center of the night the fuel begins to replenish itself, a gift of the darkness in the depths of the Grail Chalice.

I have spent many years at practicing the art of remembering my fullness. Depression used to sweep me away into a dark pit like an avalanche of ice and snow down granite slopes. Now when I catch the edge of the depression I begin to remember the fullness and to remember who I really am. The night is momentarily brief and lacks the old threat, then is followed by dawn. It's all practice. Telling you this story is practice.

Tell me, can you imagine your dying? Imagine the moment when your life recapitulates before your eyes. Could you stand up to the judgment? You see the judge doesn't stand outside. It is your eyes that have taken in all of the acts of your life, your mind that records the detail, and your mind that knows how far that you've walked from the source of life. Do you carry life's blood on your hands, fear in your heart? Could you stand up to the internal storm that blows up from the deep darkness bearing the face of the demon, bearing all that you've chosen not to see, or have you befriended it? If you can stand and smile at the center, you have a choice, a choice of where next to step. Without choice the demon casts your spirit atoms and ashes out to chaotic probability and chance dancing on the vibrating strands of nothingness. Hell is mindlessly doing the same thing over and over without choice, without even knowing that you have a choice. Practice, practice. Hold the center, remember who you really are and face the dark. The human road is the lens through which consciousness focuses itself into self-awareness and choice. It is not a mistake.

I think that something changed for Clarence King when he couldn't be the first man on the mountain. He was one of the most noted and honored men in America and yet was always looking for something else. He had been the founding director of the new United States Geological Survey, but quit after a few years to pursue other things. He began a pursuit of gold for security's sake, for predictability's sake. He became a businessman who wheeled and dealed, investing in mining schemes that drained his finances and drained his life force. King was always looking for El Dorado, the fabled city of gold, the place where one could live in a world of gleaming wealth. His dealings came tumbling down in the Panic of 1893, the avalanche that also swept away my family's wealth. The melancholy welled up into his life more than ever, pushed at the edges of his being.

King was always searching but never really finding, his fishing camp more empty than ever. He dreamed of dark skinned women with rounded bodies and earthy, fecund ways, a contrast to the high white culture in which he lived. The image of those women seemed to bring to him some sense of what he was missing, some sense of a hand extended from the dark humus of the earth bearing real life, a hope that the darkness would yield its secret. He fell in love with a young Negro nursemaid in New York City. She was the dark goddess. They ended up marrying, but out of fear of scandal he never told her his real name nor told his old friends of his new family. He kept an apartment to entertain his old friends and a separate home for his family, splitting his life into more pieces. Did he love his wife or was he in love with what she represented, the dark mystery at the core of things, the dark earth that yielded the real gold? She never knew who he was till days before his death. Because he saw her as an ideal he never knew her real being.

In 1901, at the age of fifty-nine, he lay dying of tuberculosis. He knew that he had abandoned his love of science for the lure of business and external gold. At times he would hallucinate climbing the mountains of his youth, probably remembering his bold forays into the Sierra Nevada when anything seemed possible. He could still feel something empty that had never been filled and he could never remember the question that he needed to ask. He died the day before Christmas, sedated with heroin for his pain, opium coming full circle in his life.

The night was dark and cold, but I slept soundly. Yesterday's cloud layer had lifted and I awoke on a clear morning to my first close look at the peaks all around me, of Mt. Stewart and Eagle Scout Peak rising vertically above me and of Kaweah Gap between them. The morning was cold and my fingers were numb. I could see a hint of the sun lighting the tip of a peak far down the valley toward Moro Rock and Castle Peak. Angel Wings loomed in full grandeur in the clear sky. I pulled my binoculars from my pack to scan the peaks and the gap. I could see the light begin to play about the top of Eagle Scout. As I turned back toward Angel Wings to view it close up, the morning sun began to illuminate the granite. The whiteness leaped out at me and again I felt simultaneously both dwarfed and enlarged in awe.

As I sat and ate breakfast the light began to slowly creep down the mountainside directly behind me toward camp. A slight breeze barely rippled the lake's surface, which now reflected the surrounding sheer walls of granite and ice. In the ripples thousands of lights began to dance through the slight mists that had begun to rise from the lake in the new heat of the sun. I began to scan Kaweah Gap to prepare myself for the hike up the steep ascent to the view of the Kaweah Peaks. This was it. The peaks that stood all around me were a slice of the Great Western Divide.

The light began to descend the mountainside toward the camp at a faster and faster rate. I decided to walk up the mountainside toward the light and then turned and faced into the warmth. After returning back down toward camp I savored my last few sips of green tea before preparing to depart. I headed toward the pit toilet, a luxury of sorts in the high granite, though somewhat dubious. It was a metal toilet on a claptrap deck with three low walls around it. As I warily sat on it and peered between the large gaps of the boards I felt precariously suspended over a fecal hell. Whoever had built it was totally unfamiliar with a hammer and saw. As I peered downward once more I smiled to myself, then laughed out loud. I thought, even in the far reaches of this place, maybe especially in this high place, a little craft was in order. Perhaps a little craft is always in order, building everything for other beings as if it were for God. Imagine that world. The great furniture maker and designer George Nakashima once said that if he could truly teach craft in the inner city that the ghettoes would bloom. As I looked back toward camp the sunlight had filled the granite bowl. It had become so intense that it was almost impossible to look out across the lake without being blinded.

As I left camp the heat was starting to build within the bowl. I forded the exit stream on some logs and then crossed a great stretch of slightly tilted granite. The beginning of the trail had been posted with a sign that declared, "Mountain lion habitat, solo hiking not recommended". I knew the odds were great that I would not see the mountain cat, but it was also highly possible that one might watch me from some invisible place. After crossing the granite I joined a switchback trail that began to angle steeply up the mountain. As I turned to look back I could see the nose of Moro Rock on the distant horizon. I ascended several more long switchbacks till at the northern-most reach of the last switchback I found myself as close to Angel Wings as the trail would allow. From there I could look back down valley past the towering monolith of Angel Wings and see not only a full view of Moro Rock, but also of Castle Rocks. Next to where I was standing was a giant specimen of a straight white pine that had to be at least four-and-a-half feet in diameter. As I moved on up the trail the trees turned to junipers in all manner of shapes from straight to gnarled. I turned to look back down the valley and I could see the white clouds starting to move in once more. They had already begun to obscure Moro Rock and Castle Rocks in the short time since I had last looked. I knew I had to forge ahead because the clouds would roll in early despite the glorious clear beginnings to the day. I speeded up and after a short while slowed down again. I knew that it would be a long steep hike up the mountain and that steady was better than fast. All around me were manzanita bushes full of their little apple-shaped berries and wildflowers lingering on into the fall. Lupine crowded the trail heavy with seedpods, while paintbrush and columbine poked up here and there. Behind me a finger of cloud had begun to move up River Valley.

The trail continued its switchback ascent, sometimes on a kind of organic dirt and the rest of the time on crushed and broken granite. After a while I rounded a corner to face a V-shaped chasm that yawned below and pushed back into the mountainside ahead of me. Ahead of me granite walls overhung the trail where it had been blasted out of the mountain. My boot steps began to echo eerily in the world of granite. The chasm was massively deep and fell sharply down the mountainside to the cliffs above Hamilton Lake. The trail then entered a short tunnel in the solid stone where the echoes of my passage gained in intensity. I kept wondering if I were the only one on the mountain as the lonely echoes washed over me. At the far end of the tunnel where the trail intersected the point of the V chasm I stopped to look around. Above me I could see a ridgeline that could maybe be reached by energetic boulder hopping, below me the chute spilled on down to the bright blue of Hamilton Lake at the bottom of the bowl. I could barely discern my camp on the far side of the lake.

As I continued on around the other side of the chasm I

suddenly saw something that I had missed before. Coiled against the wall was a massive steel cable. As I looked again I discerned several concrete foundation mooring points. At one time, there had been a suspension bridge strung between the sides of the chasm. I wondered what it would be like to walk the swaying bridge across the depths of this great ravine. Later I found out that the bridge had been built in 1932 but had been ripped out in an avalanche in 1937. The chasm was a giant avalanche chute and the avalanche had carried the bridge all the way down the mountain to near the lake in its tumble of liquefying ice and snow, granite and steel. The next year WPA workers had begun the arduous job of blasting the trail out of the granite face.

The trail emerged on the cliffs above Hamilton Lake where a tarn, a small steep sided lake, fed the falls that ribboned down the grey stone face to the lake below. The tarn was itself fed by a stream that emerged from Precipice Lake further up the trail. Precipice Lake itself lay at the foot of the sheer north face of Eagle Scout Peak, the setting of a famous photograph by Ansel Adams. The sheer face had been the scene of many avalanches since the glaciers had retreated thousands of years ago. Adams' photo had shown the lake in summer, its cliffs reflected in the crystal water with some snow at the foot of the cliffs. Even though it was late September as I stood there, a field of snow and ice capped the rubble field at the foot of the face and the lake itself was still frozen, having never thawed during the summer. The snow from Eagle Scout Peak extended out onto the layer of ice and half covered the lake. Across the ice a multitude of rills fell toward the lake from the snowfields high on Eagle Scout. As I listened I could hear the ice cracking as it expanded in the warmth of the day. I picked up a few stones to toss out onto the lake to test the thickness of the ice.

As I turned back to the trail to continue my push for the top, the trail suddenly disappeared beneath a wide deep snowfield that overhung the lake. A small snowmelt stream ran from beneath the bank, the snow around it colored red with lichen. The water running through the bank and under and around stones created the sound of an icy thrumming engine. I found that I had to veer around the snowfield and pick my way through the fragile meadow growth in order to continue my way toward Kaweah Gap.

Above Precipice Lake the trail encountered one small tarn lake after another connected by the small snowmelt stream. The tarn lakes formed a necklace of crystal beads that progressively became smaller as I moved upward. Finally I came to the smallest tarn, which seemed to have no other above it. There are other stream branches that feed into the Middle Fork of the Kaweah, but in my mind this tarn on the Great Western Divide was the source of the river that had defined my family and gave life and shape to my mind. I stopped for a moment in respect. I whispered a short prayer to the Whatever it Was (and Is) beneath the tarn and the granite ridge and beneath the magma deep below, a prayer to the core of things. Close above me was Kaweah Gap. I walked on up to the crest.

A stiff breeze had begun blowing up River Valley and on up through the Hamilton Lakes. I walked on over the top of the pass and down the other side about fifty feet so I could sit for a while sheltered from the wind. I got out my lunch and then my binoculars so I could look around the barren lunar landscape of the Kaweah Peaks. Below me stretched the Nine Lakes Basin, rocky and austere, punctuated by the intense blue of lakes that flowed on down to the Kern River and then around the southern tip of the Sierra to Bakersfield. This ridge was a separation of realities, the Kern an alien world to me, but the defining reality for some other person like me who had been shaped by the movement of its water. I wondered who that person might be. Would I ever meet them? Had they been able to follow the water to the source of their reality, to discover something of themselves? We all live on different streams beneath the Great Divide. Where will we meet to share our stories?

Multicolored peaks of red and black and white punctuated the ridge around the lake basin. It was a manifestation of what had led me here. Red Kaweah, Black Kaweah, Kaweah Queen. The iron stained red existed like the hemoglobin of life that connected the black and the white, the darkness and the light. The jagged shapes thrust upward from somewhere inside the gray granite monolith that formed these mountains as if to call attention to a simple and austere truth. If I remained still, maybe that truth would come and make itself known. This was not a place a place to live but it was a place for seeing. The snowmelt from the barren Kaweah Peaks fell toward the lakes below me. The snowmelt on the other side of the Kaweah Gap where I sat flowed on down the necklace of tarns to Precipice Lake and on down to the Kaweah. They poured from one to another like one grail cup filling another, constantly replenished by the ocean depths and the wind. I longed to be filled in such a fashion and to be able to pour out to another, and on and on.

The great fish had come to me in the dream and brought me on this journey and to this place. The part of me that had endured such ignominy and insult over the years wanted to believe in the special quality of the vision and the journey, but the truth is that everyone is visited by vision and asked to make the journey to the source of their nature. It's difficult to hold onto the vision, let alone remember it. Many things work against it.

Sometimes we have a moment when everything is apparent and we grasp the meaning of the deeper things, but the moment passes. We are left with an indefinite hole in our memory, a sense of something profound that slipped away and we convince ourselves that it was all delusion. Visions cannot exist as independent baubles, but need to be strung together into a whole by the practice of their lessons.

It could be said that you have to believe in yourself, but that's not it either. Believing in yourself can always fall victim to not believing in yourself and, besides, what self are you going to believe in? In the end, belief has nothing to do with it. There is seeing, practicing and remembering.

Parsifal's moment passed him by and he found himself bounced from the Grail Castle after his first visit. Left with an indefinite hole in memory he began to search again for what had slipped away. The original story ended at this point of loss, with Parsifal facing his uncertain future with no guarantee of entering the Grail castle ever again. In his own book, Robert imagined Parsifal once again entering the castle and healing the Fisher King. The original story had to end at this point because the story throws a challenge to us. Each of us has to imagine the ending for his or her own self. Can you picture yourself standing in the midst of redemption and plenty, ready to ask the question? Whom does the Grail serve? Does all of this fullness exist for the sake of my fractured being that fears and grasps, or is it meant for something larger, something all of one piece? Can you be all of one piece?

The austere jagged peaks seemed to close in toward me, the black, red and white stone seemed to whisper a thought. "Life does exist for a purpose. Say, 'Yes,' to the purpose, be connected to the purpose. Be filled with intent."

In the midst of the windy cold peaks I began to feel the sense of being all one piece again, to experience the nobility to which Robert had referred. I knew that this sense of deep inner nobility was the real gold in the midst of this world of the Living Dead where we try to possess gold in order to feel noble. I was both Parsifal and the Fisher King. When the two came together, there was just "who I really am." I had somehow drawn the opposites together. In the little church with the false front long ago I had been too small to hold the immensity of the question and the answer. At the headwaters of my family's reality in this new world I could feel my grandfather's spirit around me. These were the peaks that had looked over my shoulder during my youth and sustained me. For me this was the land of the Grandfather Spirit and I could feel its intent. Would I be able to carry on the intent of this spirit, the intent of life itself, to live with conscious purpose and conscious connection? I had drifted through so much of my portion of life.

This whole landscape spread before me was a grand panorama of my mind made so clear that any fool could see. There was no great vision, there were no gods leaping from behind granite boulders, just the sense of commitment to life and to giving voice to that which has no voice. I wondered how I would remember this sense of purpose? In the Great Valley below, people claimed salvation by reading a book and believing that a mountain existed, even though the mountains themselves were gone from view behind the smog of commerce and living. The belief is but a rumor of God, a rumor of the mountain, a rumor of the deeper things. How many of them would shake off the torpor and living deadness to go to the source, to go to the mountain for themselves? Go to the mountain, cease believing and begin knowing. The mountain is always there, free of creed or mantra or sutra or scripture. Any fisherman or farm boy or farm girl or fatherless child can climb the mountain and see. The great divide in our minds, our separation from who we really are, happens when we fail to assume the responsibility for our own spiritual destiny. We want someone or something else to save us, to guarantee our destiny. Full life is more than a recipe.

Great spirituality is not about great leaps of faith. Rather it is about taking the many small steps along the road that you know to be right.

Would I find allies in my intent? I thought of my family back home in Santa Barbara. I knew that that being part of this family was a gift of the Grandparents and that this gift would help sustain me.

As I turned to look behind, a wispy cold finger of fog snaked over Kaweah Gap fifty feet above me and began to gesture that my moment was finished. I quickly gathered up my lunch and binoculars, put them into my fanny pack and turned to go. My first step over the ridge carried me down into the dense pea soup fog, a fog that again reminded me of the dank tule fogs of my childhood. My doubt began to once more close in and work at decreasing the size of my mind. Would the moment on the mountaintop be just another bauble? I descended past the necklace of small tarns, the muffled slight gurgle of water flowing from tarn to tarn the only sound other than my boots. As I got back to the upper end of Precipice Lake I encountered a block of red granite along the trail that was a foot taller than me. It had a natural calligraphy of a contrasting red on its uphill face. The calligraphy was organic, oak-like, fetal and somehow seemed to encapsulate my experience. As I looked toward the lake I could no longer see a sign of Eagle Scout Peak on the other side. In fact I could only see the nearest shore of the lake.

As I walked I tried to remember the feeling of nobility and the feeling of having a larger mind. With the memory, I pushed back at the inner fog that threatened to grip me as it always had. I passed the sterile tarn lake at the head of the waterfall and moved down onto the switchbacks that wound across the granite face above Upper Hamilton. Around me in the fog I could see plants heavy with seedpods ready to fall to the ground beneath winter snows. Life was always pushing its way even into the heights like fingers of consciousness that push into the unconscious.

I passed the coiled cable of the old suspension bridge and entered the tunnel, passing from the dense fog into the darkness and back into the fog. The echoing sound of my muffled boot steps gave me the eerie sense that I was being followed. I was still being stalked by the old demon, though it had lost power. It kept whispering at me, telling me to lose my intent, to go back to numb drifting and vague hopes. I countered by remembering my daughter and how I had met her when she was five. She had shyly reached up and placed her hand in mine as if she knew that I was going to be around for a long time.

I descended into a cold and wet camp in late afternoon and could see, at most, thirty feet out onto the lake. I shed my pack and put on warmer clothes, then sat on a rock near the lake edge. I needed something—a sign—one last thing to show me that I was not suffering delusions, that my fractured ego was not playing tricks, so I said a quick prayer.

Over time I have come to a different understanding of prayer. Prayer is not imploring, begging and groveling before some demanding God. What infinite manner of thing could possibly need you or me to implore, grovel and beg? My prayer is like this: In my mind I see what is really needed and then gently extend my ki, my silver current of salmon energy in that direction. Beseeching, begging and imploring is like trying to muscle and twist God to my point of view, like a child trying to get its own small way.

Around me the mist slowly rose to reveal the outline of the lake and the small island. Then suddenly the cloud began to lift faster and start to separate till I could see all of Eagle Scout Peak reflecting the western late afternoon sun, the silver waterfall strand gleaming and the reflection of the granite mountain in the water before me. The mountain stood revealed before me for fifteen to twenty minutes bathed in low raking autumn light before the clouds once more came to meet the lake. The clouds, the mountains, the lake. The chill returned. If I had asked for more I would have been greedy. The rest was up to me.

I am walking through the mountains with an older man. We see another older man along the trail and approach him. As we approach the man, he looks carefully at me and then smiles at the old man with me and says, "I see he's now finally enlightened." I feel embarrassed at such an assessment, but then begin to search my consciousness. I finally begin to agree with the old stranger because the understanding has come on me so slowly over such a long period of time that it has become just a mundane, everyday part of my being. It is nothing special and so I haven't noticed.

Return

Even when daylight comes your task is not ended. You have merely found that you have the courage to face life and to live with purpose. When you earn a black belt, it is not time to stop practice. It is only the beginning.

The night before I left Upper Hamilton I dreamt that my daughter and I had discovered a nest of small immature doves in the garage entry of my grandparent's farmhouse. One had fallen out so we picked it up and returned it to its nest.

The scene changed and suddenly the nest was in a box in the camper shell of my pickup truck. The doves seemed a little scared but I began to soothe them. I found some earthworms in the corner of the pickup bed and gently put a dove near it. It attacked the worm with gusto.

Again the scene changed and I found myself with a large wolf that I had acquired. It had killed my dog, but I felt no threat. Other people, though, felt that it was a threat to the doves. As the wolf stretched at my

feet I knew it had its wolf nature, its wolf ways, but I
still felt protective of it. I knew somehow I had to find
a way to incorporate both the wolf and the doves into
my life.

When I studied T'ai Chi my teacher was an eighty-year-old Chinese man. He explained that with his right hand he could heal, but his left hand could kill. If he had denied his capacity for violence, he would have lost access to a large part of the energy used for healing. So many people who start down the spiritual road become wimpy shells. They call this state "love", afraid to look their own violence in the eye and transform its energy. This is one of the traps along the way.

There is no magic bullet that will end my violence. Each day the flies of violent thoughts and impulses rise from the deep, ancient recess of my brain and I have to snatch them in midair and transform them, do the alchemical dance. Yes, I can kill, but today I find no need to. There is always constant awareness of who I am and what I am doing here. Some days I am less aware than others. Some days on the mat are better than others. As we left T'ai Chi class the teacher would simply say, "Practice, practice." There is only practice and being aware of the change.

If you make it through this night what will you practice to maintain your awareness of who you really are? What will you do to bring you to your larger mind, till life within the larger mind is an everyday mundane experience hardly worthy of comment? Who will you touch and how? There is room in the world for everyone to be noble with none left behind. What would this world look like with everyone guided by an inner awareness of their own depths and their own nobility? Those whose lives and livelihoods depend on telling others what to do would view this as chaotic and anarchic and so fear it, but there is an unseen order below the obvious, a larger mind that weaves the fabric. Sadly we don't know how to trust that order. There are those who will always seek to impose their own small will in order to contain the knowledge of the deeper things and to forcibly graffiti their names on the stones of history. The smaller and more fractured a person's mind, the more they will seek to impose order in order to feel large and the more they will seek to claim that they know God's will for your life. A large mind simply is, guided by its own knowing, and reaches out to gently touch whomever it can.

When I arose the last morning at Upper Hamilton, there was ice on my tent. As I packed up camp to leave the lake in the frozen chill, I knew I was neither my father nor the Buddha. I was going back to my family to practice my awareness, not abandoning them. It would have been a wonderful thing for Christianity if Jesus had had children. By making him God he was removed from human experience, removed from human attainment. In order to get to Christ one has to go through verses and interpretations, churches and cathedrals, ministers and priests. The real unburdened Christ represents a certain experience of life, a certain connection to the depth of life that is open to anyone. It is a simple love for being alive, a love for the process of life. This experience, this love, is revolutionary. I knew that I was just a heretic. The original meaning of heretic was "one who has made a choice." I dream that we all become enlightened heretics inhabiting this great planet as it swings through the stars. I had gone to the mountain and was going home, like a new salmon headed toward the sea. If I practiced and remembered I would always be able to return to the mountain above the Great Western Divide.

I don't worship Christ, but admire him. He is someone you meet along the way. You sit, have tea, meet eyebrow to eyebrow and touch minds. You smile and share the great view.

Whom does the Grail serve? It serves a larger mind that then pours out into pools that cascade on down the mountainside and into the valley. If I could have, I would have reached out to touch Clarence King and to show him the real gold that was in the Sierra Nevada. I would have touched my father and grandfather and grandmother, Dutch Bill and all my ancestors. I was there because of all their efforts both small and large, both fractured and whole. If I could have I also would have reached out to touch the corporate farmers of the Tulare Lake bottom and shown them the heart that still beats beneath the white alkaline encrusted place and shown them the spirits that still swim over the surface of the dried out land. If I could I would have shown them who they really are.

If you can truly taste the air within each breath, then you cannot pollute the air. If you can truly feel the earth beneath your feet, then you cannot desecrate the ground. If you can really feel your true life, then you can no longer curse life or seek to abuse it. You can no longer invent excuses and rationalizations to abuse and kill others in the name of God.

As I walked down the trail by Lower Hamilton I passed again beneath the vertical presence of Angel Wings and Valhalla. I paused to say a brief thanks and moved on, not wanting to overstay my welcome. As I passed through the jungle of plants and vines near the top of the waterfalls, three ripe wild raspberries appeared on a vine next to the path. They were so ripe that they fell into my hand, staining my fingers red. I thought of the iron rich, blood red stains of the Kaweah Peaks as I savored their sweetness, then moved on along the trail.

As I passed by one of the pools at the top of the falls a nine-to ten-inch trout fled ten feet back up the stream, broke the surface in the shallows and then dove to hide in the dark shadows of tree roots exposed by the flowing water. I began my descent down the switchbacks and back through the manzanita land of the guardian lizards and the tailless lizard king.

The way back was mostly all descent, so I pushed on quickly. As I arrived back at Bearpaw Meadow I decided not to spend the night in the vast and dusty empty camp. I moved on down the mountain to a camp at Buck's Creek. The campsite was set in a thicket that contained thickets of ripened chokecherries. All around me piles of red stained scat proclaimed that this was bear central and that this was their deli. I was so tired that I could move no further down the trail so I had to stop and set up camp. The good thing was that after several nights in the high granite I would now be able to make a campfire to meet the night.

The trip that I had undertaken was neither dangerous nor particularly physically hard, but I was exhausted nevertheless. What gave the trip significance was that it was an expression of clear intent. I was motivated by something deep and mysterious to take the journey. As I sat on the bear box I was pervaded by the tiredness. When I exist in small and fractured mind, tiredness and pain become entries to a dark whirlpool of depression and the sum total of all my failures. As Freud said, "Sometimes a cigar is just a cigar." I let tiredness just be tiredness with no further judgment.

After a quick dinner I lit a campfire where I could sit and write. I was hungry for companionship, would have loved to talk someone about the mountains and the trees. I also missed my family. I wondered if I would be as tongue tied as ever in expressing my love to Barbara. It felt like something always stopped me from saying the deep things. In the midst of the thoughts I realized that this Buck's Creek day was also my mother's birthday, a day to remember her birth into this landscape. I put out the fire so that I could get a long night's sleep for the last day.

I come upon several men who are fighting, so I decide to break it up by challenging one of the men to an arm wrestling contest. I want to see if I can use the ki energy without using any muscle. We sit down and after relaxing my arm and toying with him for a bit I turn his arm over and throw him back through the wall. He keeps flying back through wall after wall after wall, breaking them down. People go to look for him but don't find him, though I know that he is indeed okay. Several men want to know how I did what I did. A boy is watching and, impressed with the act, wants to learn how. I look around and see a passive audience that doesn't seem to react to anything surrounds us. I don't mind though. What seems to be of the greatest importance is the relationship with the boy. We walk away together.

My journey has mostly been solitary, except for my present family and the closest friends. It has been difficult to share my deepest experience with very many people. I live something far larger now in my spirit and in my personal life but am still lonely. Sometimes the loneliness feels as if it could crush the largeness of my being. It is my last great demon. I simply look for a circle of friends, friends who see, friends who live in awe. I envision us together in a larger place, living with larger minds. I envision us reclaiming our nobility, our largeness of being and our intent. I envision us reclaiming ourselves as a people and a country so that we can see, practice and remember. I see us living an everyday largeness that can spill out and flow down to touch those that long to be touched. Christ is not returning if you don't arrive, the coming Buddha Maitreya is only your discovery of yourself. True religion is not about ministers and priests. It's really about friends walking the road together. Companionship, laughter and shared awe. Don't give away your real gold, your consciousness, to others to finance their empires of power.

Organized religion exists for the sake of enforced common experience, but not for true spirituality. The God that you read about is not the God you'll find. In the end organized religion is the way of the spiritually lazy or spiritually afraid person, a person addicted to the comfort of certainty and afraid of the nature of evolution and change. Changes, changes, suddenly there were changes. We get to choose what we are to become, the fruit of the tree in the garden. We are taught that we are children of God needing to be led, the shepherd and his flock. We thirst to be loved. Sheep are not very intelligent. We have to grow up to be adults of God, responsible for making wise choices and willing to extend love and compassion, overflowing our containers. Get off your butt and quit hoping for salvation, just go to the mountain in the mind, light a campfire, look into the ugly face and be surprised. While we wait for deliverance we don't take care of the moment and we lose the moment forever. We also lose the earth where we live.

Not long after daybreak I finished my oatmeal and set out on the trail to head back out the canyon of the Middle Fork of the Kaweah. Soon Castle Rocks, the Undertakers, loomed before me and dominated my view, and then I could see the outline of Moro Rock. I paused at Mehrten Creek to once again consider my family then moved on toward home. Along the trail I met a young man in his early twenties loaded with an eighty-five-pound pack full of camera gear. I wished him well, wondering if he was going to try to capture the ineffable or to meet it. As I closed in on Moro Rock and Crescent Meadow the breeze shifted to blow my way from down canyon. I thought that I heard a hymn being sung, then the breeze shifted and it was gone. Again I heard voices. What were they singing, then gone once more. I decided that I was just too tired and that I was hearing only what I wanted to hear.

I rounded the edge of Crescent Meadow and looked about to see if there was a church service of some kind, but saw only scattered clusters of Chinese people standing around talking, laughing. In the wide center divider in the parking lot an old man was doing some form of Chi Gong to raise his Chi and nearby another man did T'ai Chi. I stowed my pack in the truck with a feeling of tiredness and relief, then pulled out my keys to leave. On a sudden whim I went over to the nearest person, a woman, and explained that I thought I had heard singing. Did she know anything about it? She smiled and said they were a church from Los Angeles and called themselves "Spirit of Life." I smiled back as we bowed to each other, then I left.

I knew that I couldn't leave the area without climbing Moro Rock one more time. As I climbed the 350 steps to the top I had to marvel once more about Robert's ability to climb these steps. In my mind that effort seemed to surpass anything that I had done. I hoped that I had completed something for him, completed some vague yearning to know what lie in the peaks out on the eastern horizon. Some part of me still wanted him to be waiting at the top. As I reached the top of the rock I could see the outline of a quarter-becoming-half moon in the still day lit sky. I surveyed the vista for a while and studied the peaks and passes where I had been, the ridge of granite that had risen from the bottom of the sea and would one day wear down. A raven hovered in the air in the thermals that moved up the face of the rock, soared close, then disappeared.

As I started to descend the stairs, I could hear another raven laughing in the distance up canyon along the trail where I had just been, somewhere near the point where I had first heard the singing. Near the bottom portion of the stairs, there is an outline map that shows the range of the Great Western Divide and names the peaks on the horizon. An old Chinese man stood near the map. As I began to pass he gestured to me and asked what the map and the mountains meant, so I stopped and began to try and explain to him the nature of the Great Western Divide.

The highest good is like water.
Water gives life to the ten thousand things and does
not strive.
It flows in the places that men reject and so is like the Tao.
In dwelling, be close to the land.
In meditation, go deep in the heart.
In dealing with others, be gentle and kind.
In speech be true.
In ruling, be just.
In daily life, be competent.
In action, be aware of the time and the season.
No fight: No blame.

—Lao Tsu

Home

I see the sun beginning to rise over the granite peaks to the east. You haven't really lived until you've seen the morning sun reflecting off a high snowy peak, then gradually work its way down the mountain to you. Along the way each tree and rock is touched with light and comes to life, till finally the whole bowl of granite is filled with the intensity of the day.

It's now time for me to leave. It has been ten years since I took the journey to the Great Western Divide and it is only now that I tell it. My life is always my laboratory and I can speak of no more than I am. I had to know if I could be a good parent and partner, that my daughter would be happy and loved but also strong and kind. It hasn't always been easy, but it has been good practice. This is the fruit of my life, the fruit of my intent. That is the way that it's been and now I can tell you the story without fear of lying. It is also time for my daughter to hear this story so that she can learn from it what she may as she becomes an adult in this mysterious world.

In *Zen Mind, Beginner's Mind*, Shunryu Suzuki said, "To give your sheep or cow a large spacious meadow is the way to control him. So it is with people: first let them do what they want, and watch them. This is the best policy. To ignore them is not good; that is the worst policy. The second worst is trying to control them. The best one is to watch them, just to watch them, without trying to control them." He was also speaking of the mind.

When I was once asked how I could be such a successful parent with the history that I had had to endure, I replied, "I was always present for my daughter and I gave her a large pasture. Her pasture was always slightly larger than her reach so that she never felt imprisoned. She always knew that I loved her."

Do you lecture your children, or do you teach them how to touch the "spirit of life" by your example? The morality to be taught is not based in what you believe, but rather in living who you really are.

Since my return the course of my life has followed a strange logic that I couldn't always see in the moment. My life began to unfold without striving if I listened deeply, as if I were finally freed of some family curse and my father and Dutch Bill were laid to rest. The times that I became impatient and decided to try and make things happen ended in terrible failure. I would be cast back into the deep crack in the ground, small and afraid. But during this time I also began to develop my greatest power. That power is the ability to look inside and know the right thing to do and do it, no matter how I feel, no matter what fear tries to grip my body and spirit.

When I returned our daughter was in the sixth grade. We wanted her to have a fuller experience of life than we knew she would receive the next year at the local junior highs, but we had no idea what that could be. During February a friend came by and told us of a local private middle school where they wanted to send their son. It had outdoor trips of bicycling, backpacking and camping three times a year in order for the kids to learn self-reliance, courage and community. We knew that this was where our daughter belonged even though we had no idea where the money would come from. But I was as sure of the decision to send her as I was of meeting her mother years before when I sat at my grandparent's grave. I was sure, even though my income was erratic and I knew that my days as a carpenter were due to come to an end.

She thrived at the school, coming home every day singing. There is no greater gift than this, than to hear your child singing with joy every day. I felt no sacrifice and there was no debt for her to repay, nothing to be held over her head. Her joy was all. As I watched what happened at the school I knew that I wanted to return to education at this school, that I would be able to integrate my love of the outdoors. At the end of her first school year I was offered a job as an instructor of mathematics. I was even able to create my own midyear trip, cross-country skiing in the winter forest on the rim above Yosemite Valley. I have had a great opportunity to be valuable and needed.

Yet, I know that even this great and good thing with my students is due to come to an end, just as parenthood has come to its natural end. My father was a carpenter and my mother was a teacher. I have done these jobs well, but I have not yet fully lived the life that I am here to live. This story points the way, but I don't yet know the timing or all of the details. The big story cannot be forced, and everything has its own pace and time. I haven't been to Mt. Whitney yet, but I will someday soon.

On Christmas Day a year or so ago my family was cross-country skiing in the High Sierra near Lake Tahoe. We left in a snowstorm with Interstate 80 icy and slick. Trees hung impossibly heavy with snow. The snow followed us down to between three and four thousand feet where we began to emerge from the storm. Out on the western horizon we could see the edge of another approaching storm.

As we came into Auburn and could look out across the Great Valley the sky directly overhead cleared and the sun began to descend behind the approaching storm. As we passed through Sacramento the clouds began to become illuminated by the setting sun and take on a multitude of colors. The shapes of the clouds seemed to be portals to another world as they gradually changed configuration in the light.

We left Sacramento and crossed the bridge over the remaining wetlands where the valley of the San Joaquin becomes the valley of the Sacramento. The sun dipped beneath the clouds and lit them from below. The glow extended across the known universe and into the unknown. The wetlands reflected the sun, the clouds and the hills that surround the Delta and Suisun Bay. Everything was united once more in its myriad manifestations. I knew that my father's grave along the Carquinez Strait was bathed in this light. The moment was a vision for the return of Tulare Lake and the central San Joaquin into the landscape of our mind made real, with the sunlight reflecting across the expanse of water. This is how it could be. The ninety-mile glint of silver could return if we wanted it to, if we humbly asked, if we humbly set ourselves to the task. It was as if the great fish spirit of the lake had chosen to come back to life for a moment in this time and this place. This illumination is how the mind can truly be. The glorious color faded into a multiplicity of shades of gray and black, then slipped back into Christmas night.

The day I finished this story I rode my bicycle out to the bluffs overlooking the Pacific to watch the setting sun. Several hundred feet below me the beach stretched out toward the sea at low tide. The blue-green sea was calm and rippled by a slight wind. A hundred yards from shore I caught a flash of movement and dolphins began to break the surface on a leisurely swim westward along the shore into the setting sun. As I watched, they doubled back and began to swim in circles toward the shore below me. Welcome back. A few languidly stretched on the surface as one thrust straight up out of the water and looked around. Welcome back. The changelings slowly circled away into the west till they crossed the sun. I watched till my eyes could no longer bear the light, then left for home.

Look out into the sunlight now as it illuminates this mysterious world and the mystery of being. Imagine being fearless as you climb its peaks, plumb its depths, explore its nuance and restore its meaning. All of this is yours, the landscape of your real mind.

Speak

Who will speak for the ground outside
waterlogged after two weeks of constant rain,
the water seeping down to aquifers
emptied by years of drought
and decades of greed,
if not me, then who?
Who will air the strivings of the new grass,
the paper white narcissus backdropped

by the new redwood fence,
if not me, then who?
What of the air
heavy with the sweet flower smell
burdened by the sounds of too many cars
on the U.S. highway a half-mile away.
what of my daughter's child thoughts,
her delight in her cats,
my erotic thoughts of her mother,
if not me, then who?
This house, this family burdened by debts
to things that we did not create, this
neighborhood uneasy with the future,
fearful of its visionless past.
Lovers contemplate their bodies,
the chance for a child, a life together
without any knowledge of the true nature of things.
And my parents and grandparents dirtied
and torn by forces with no human face.
And our Elders, the knowledge, the visions of the true ways
slaughtered for a greed and a power,
an arrogance that has no human face,
if not me, then who?
Who will give voice to this breath, this moment,
and in this moment a glimpse
of an old man, an old woman
who beckon me to them and say,
speak
the words will come to you,
just hold to the vision and speak.

This is my understanding of things, my imperfect rendering of the bottom of the sea, of you and all the other faces of humanity. If this understanding fills you, then pour it out to another. And on and on. Let the Tao pour from depths of the Grail. You are what you are able to perceive.

I'll say one thing. The gold that you find will show you that you are really no Buddhist, no Muslim, Hindu or Christian. You are simply and fully a human being. How wonderful. But, be warned. It is not easy being a human being in a world of gods and sinners. This is no wishy-washy thing.

"All right, noble person, here is your face shown to you – straight and without editing. Please take it as soon as you can and keep faith and courage in the meantime.

Please have my faith and respect in you."

This is the vision of your mind. What will you do with such a thing? There is much work to be done.

I know an old man that I have met sometime in the past is dying. I am saddened because I know there is still something to be learned from him. I want to go find him and hope I get there before he dies. Somehow I feel needed. When I find the old man's house and enter I see his wife standing and waiting. He is lying on a table and is in spasms. His head seems fine, but his body is skinny and contorts with each spasm. The body folds over like paper and flips around.

I go over to catch the old man in my arms as he starts to bounce off the table. I catch his head and cradle him before he hits the hard floor. My arms seem

*strong and the catch seems effortless. I put him back on
the table. Instead of dying, to my surprise the old man
suddenly sits up, reaches for his pipe and tobacco, then
begins to smoke. He says, "This wasn't as bad as the
last one," then smiles.*

*My brother has been standing silently in the
shadows nearby, finally freed from his confinement
within the crack in the ground. We look at each other
and begin to smile broadly, then we begin to laugh as
we set out into the world together.*

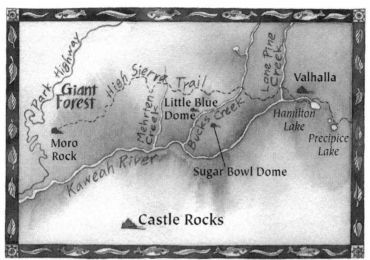

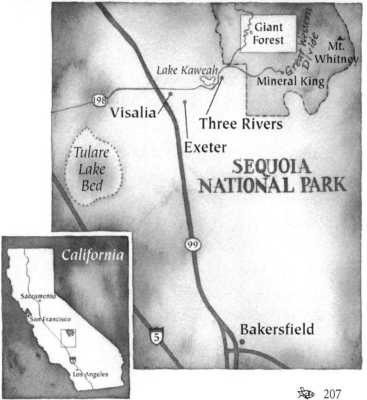

Acknowledgments

For the people:
> My mother Marie, who has known much sorrow,
> Barbara and our daughter, Danica, I bow to them,
> Davis TeSelle, we touch foreheads across a continent.

For those who encouraged my writing when all seemed a loss:
> Shelley Lowenkopf,
> Michael Madden.

For those who taught and encouraged me:
> Robert Blakemore, in memoriam,
> Robert A. Johnson, Gournamond in the flesh.

For my ancestors:
> Harry and Myrtle Mehrten, sweet tears of sadness that
> you're gone,
> Dutch Bill Mehrten,
> F. Norwood Spivey, my father, may he find peace.

For places:
> The Kaweah River and the Great Western Divide, the Sierra,
> Tulare Lake, whose fish spirits dwell in me,
> the San Joaquin Valley, rich soils and untapped spiritual
> wealth, may you recover in time.

For further support:

Gail Kearns, for editorial help and guidance,

Chris Nolt, for design help and a sweet presence,

Jane English, for kind words,

Tom Killion, for allowing a stranger to appropriate his art,

Jeremy Taylor, for teaching me about the world of dreams.

For sources:

"Coyote Genesis" was first published in *The Sun*, January, 1997

Feng, Gia-fu and Jane English. *Tao Te Ching*/Lao Tsu. New York: Vintage Books, 1972

Jackson, Louise. *Beulah: A Biography of the Mineral King Valley of California*. Tucson: Westernlore Press, 1988

Homer, Rodney Prestage, Editor. *Mehrtens of the San Joaquin Newsletter*, Porterville, CA

Johnson, Robert A. *He: Understanding Masculine Psychology*, Revised Edition. New York: Harper and Row, 1989

King, Clarence. *Mountaineering in the Sierra Nevada*. Lincoln: University of Nebraska Press, 1970

Latta, Frank. *Handbook of Yokuts Indians.* Exeter, CA: Brewer's Historical Press, 1999

Lufkin, Allan. *California's Salmon and Steelhead*. Berkeley: University of California Press, 1991

Wilkins, Thurman. *Clarence King: A Biography*. New York: The Macmillan Company, 1958

For all of this, I am grateful.